# DBT FOR DATING WORKBOOK

MINDFULNESS AND EMOTIONAL SKILLS
FOR SENSITIVE SINGLES

Vanessa Claire Soleil

Un Oeuf Press

Cary, North Carolina

Vanessa Claire Soleil/Un Oeuf Press
vanessascounseling.com

DBT for Dating Workbook: Mindfulness and Emotional Skills for Sensitive Singles/ Vanessa Claire Soleil. —1st ed.
ISBN 979-8-9870956-2-1

*Dedicated to my mom.*
*Thank you for teaching me how to read*
*and always encouraging my writing.*

# CONTENTS

# INTRODUCTION

**Dating is hard!**

Non-stop swiping that feels more like a videogame than a relational experience. Texting that never leads to a date. Awkward first dates that seem like job interviews. The letdown of unrequited feelings. Because all of this and more, the time and energy required to find a love match makes dating an emotionally demanding and draining process.

While dating has always had its challenges, anecdotally, dating seems to have gotten even harder in the past few years. If it's the pandemic that has caused people to forget social niceties and conversational skills, the background anxiety of years fraught with economic precarity and political polarization, or the increasing reliance on dating apps that allow us to behave in ways we never would in person, who knows?! Maybe it's all these factors converging to make dating such a grueling, frustrating, disheartening, disappointing and even destabilizing process for so many.

Yet, humans are wired to bond and attach. Most of us yearn for love, intimacy, and companionship. Unless from a community or culture where arranged marriage is the norm, dating, so far, seems to be the best way to get there. If we have to date to find love, it's helpful to find ways to take care of ourselves, stay centered, and make wise decisions along the way.

I wrote this workbook for my fellow romantics out there, for those who long for a loving relationship that lasts, who dream of a committed, fun, and sexually fulfilling partnership and of sharing life's memorable moments with a best friend. You are the kind of person who can be loyal, giving, and are ready to compromise and be someone's teammate. Sometimes, though, you lack the skills required to find a good match. You may need to practice more resiliency to cope with the highs and lows of the dating process and take on a wider, and wiser, perspective when looking to create and sustain healthy relationships.

If you want a supportive guide by your side as you learn to steady yourself and adeptly ride the emotional waves of modern dating, this workbook is for you. If you want to avoid investing in what looks like a loving relationship, only to find out, months, years, and many tears too late, that your significant other is not a quality partner, this workbook can help.

Dating can lead to a fulfilling and satisfying connection and delightful romantic feelings. It can also stir up insecurities, tax our patience, and remind us how alone we feel when a date or budding relationship goes awry. We can feel lost in confusion over mixed signals, on a roller coaster of hopeful highs and ghosting lows. We can get misled into unhealthy situations by those seductive highs and then crushed by the disappointments of those lows.

For some who are particularly sensitive, dating can touch in on tender pain points that remind you of earlier times in your life when you have felt unloved or unworthy. This can send you spiraling into thoughts about your flaws and fears of being alone "forever" or activate old stories of shame and abandonment. For others of you, you may feel on edge about losing yourself and your independence in a relationship, ending up with the wrong person, or worry that you will disappoint others or not be a good partner. Whichever your tendency, DBT skills can guide you through these patterns and help you express your needs.

This workbook is also for you if you tend to get swept up in the strong emotions of a new connection. In the haze of the honeymoon stage, we often commit to people who have not yet actually earned our trust and devotion. Not to say it won't be earned, but early on there hasn't been sufficient time to know whether love and commitment are appropriate. If you tend to throw yourself completely into a new relationship or are ready to self-sacrifice to prove your love within days or weeks of meeting someone, this likely means you've been overtaken by the powerful chemical cocktail of what's known as limerence.

**This is your brain on lust.**

Several years ago, I had the ecstatic experience of falling in love with someone. It was a mutual infatuation, with us gazing into each other's eyes, boldly declaring our amorous feelings only a few weeks in, writing love notes to each other every day. This person seemed to be everything I was looking for—they were intelligent, fun, communicative, self-aware, supportive, valued their friendships, and they also saw and appreciated my strengths. At least this is how it seemed.

Once I was already emotionally invested in an idealized version of this person, I became unwilling to see and integrate any negative qualities that started to emerge several months into our relationship. Instead of updating my picture of them to a more accurate view, I clung onto the idea of this person that I had created during the honeymoon stage of our connection. I kept them on a pedestal and explained away as an exception self-centered and hurtful behaviors or believed them when they told me that their anger, defensiveness, and distance were somehow my fault. When friends expressed concerns, I had excuses and explanations about why our situation was unique. I did this for years until it culminated in callous discarding behaviors, complete with gaslighting.

It is easier for us to remember to use mindfulness skills when we are feeling depressed or anxious, but even our positive emotions can mislead us. It is important to look more closely at our feelings of love, excitement, and hope, to make sure they are based on genuine vulnerable connection and consistent mutual support. Sometimes what can feel like excitement is our nervous system in a heightened state due to receiving intermittent affection. A dynamic with back-and-forth cycles of closeness and distance, support and abandonment, idealization and devaluation is especially addictive to the brain. It is often these relationships—where someone is sometimes loving and sometimes rejecting, that are the trickiest to suss out and the hardest to leave.

Had I used the skills and steps outlined in this workbook, I would have slowed down and made different choices based on whom I was getting to know over time, rather than flinging myself fully into a codependent dynamic with someone I assumed I knew. I could have avoided a lot of pain if I had used my DBT skills more diligently. I have been inspired by my own experience to write a workbook with skills that can help you protect yourself and choose a mate with whom you can build a healthy and loving relationship.

**Why I wrote this workbook.**

There are DBT guidebooks for folks who are already in relationship, to reduce conflict and improve communication, and there are DBT workbooks for dealing with anxiety, depression, anger, or for living with diagnoses of borderline personality disorder (BPD), and post-traumatic stress disorder (PTSD), for instance. However, dating can be a particularly vulnerable and fraught experience for many. What you will find here is DBT adapted for specific situations and attachment experiences that come up in the dating process.

DBT has benefitted me so much ever since I joined a skills group as a patient in 2012. Ten years later, I am a Licensed Clinical Mental Health Counselor (LCMHC) in North Carolina and Provisional Licensed Professional Counselor in (LPC) Pennsylvania, facilitating my own DBT groups. DBT has become such an integral part of my life that I often use the skills without thinking about it. I have come to rely on many of the skills like I do breathing. Other times, I need to pull out worksheets and refresh myself on tools I can use when things feel hard. As I have shared, there were times, as well, when I didn't even think to use

DBT skills, but later regretted it. We psychotherapists are human and fallible, indeed. I think my personal experience with and commitment to using DBT skills will help make this book more relatable and effective.

In the past, I often unintentionally sabotaged and undermined attempts to connect by having poor boundaries, not communicating well, and putting my emotions onto someone else instead of managing my own experience. Too often, my inability to tolerate the natural highs and lows of dating would lead me to internalize and interpret the lows as messages about my worth or to misinterpret the highs of anxious adrenaline spikes due to someone's unavailability as positive excitement. I sometimes let my emotions drive my decisions and ended in up in relationships that were either not a good fit, or downright toxic. For anyone who struggles with dating and relationships, I wrote this book for you, because this has been my journey, too. I know how challenging it can be and want to share the tools that have helped me.

So, if you ever...

- obsess about dating
- find yourself scanning any social event looking for "the one"
- fixate about the person you are dating, and wonder what the person thinks of you more than you consider what you like about them and whether they are a good match
- focus on finding love to feel less lonely, rather than on giving love to feel more connected
- override your intuition to make things work
- alter or censor yourself to be liked
- hold back on stating what you want or need to keep the relationship going
- get attached quickly
- give away your power and worth to the relationship
- ignore red flags and tolerate inappropriate, unkind, or harmful behavior to preserve the relationship
- get disillusioned quickly

- find yourself blaming others for being single or having failed relationships
- find yourself despairing when a date or relationship doesn't work out
- find yourself making black and white totalizing statements like "I will always be alone," "I'll never find someone," "No one is good enough for me"
- find yourself personalizing the experience of unrequited feelings
- wait anxiously to hear from your date, and cannot feel settled or calm until you do
- end up getting in relationships that reenact previous experiences of rejection and abandonment

...then this workbook has something to offer you.

**What is DBT?**

Many of you picking up this book will have already experienced the wonderful benefits of the therapeutic program known as Dialectical Behavior Therapy, or DBT. If you've participated in a DBT group or followed a skills workbook before, that will certainly make the content here easy to understand and use. No worries, though, for those new to DBT, I will break down and explain the skills so that this workbook is still accessible and supportive wherever you are in your healing journey.

Dialectical Behavior Therapy (DBT) is a skills-based therapy system that Marsha Linehan developed throughout the 1970s to enhance traditional models of Cognitive Behavior Therapy, or CBT.[1] CBT focuses on changing thoughts and behaviors to change emotions. Linehan worked with clients who didn't always respond well to CBT and its focus on change. Being told to change our thoughts to feel better can feel disempowering and dismissive, since often, emotions are so potent that trying to even hear our thoughts, much less approach them in a rational way to challenge them, can feel impossible. We also often experience our emotions as so real, and want those feelings validated instead of challenged or to be told they are caused by "distorted" thinking. Linehan started incorporating more of a validating, emotion-centered lens into her approach that emphasized not only change, but also acceptance. There are many "dialectics" in DBT--that is, opposites that are reconciled to create something new. I have already mentioned the most crucial dialectic in DBT: that of acceptance and change. In DBT, we learn to accept life, ourselves, and our emotions, while also doing what we can to make positive changes towards living a more meaningful, content, and effective life. DBT can be applied to all aspects of life to create a life we are fully and authentically participating in.

This paradigm can inform how we date—to allow us to be with ourselves and others as we are now, acknowledge the inherent risks, rejections, and rewards of the process, while we take steps towards our goals and improve our strategies to better connect with others and discern who is and is not a fit for us. Linehan called DBT a "life improvement program."[2] Is there anything more central to life than our relationships? And if dating is an important way we find and co-create relationships, the skills taught here can help us improve our lives.

DBT consists of 4 modules with different content areas and was one the earliest therapy modalities to place mindfulness at its center.

The modules focused on change are:

**Emotion Regulation**—These skills help us identify and express our emotions, reduce the intensity and frequency of painful emotions, and create a life with positive experiences that lead to more pleasant and nourishing emotions.

**Interpersonal Effectiveness**—With these strategies we can learn to be more effective communicators and focus on meeting goals while also having healthy relationships with ourselves and others.

The modules focused on acceptance are:

**Mindfulness**—Inspired by Buddhist traditions, DBT teaches mindfulness so we can be more fully ourselves rather than react to life out of conditioned habits, and so we can reduce suffering caused by judging life, ourselves, and others.

**Distress Tolerance**—Sometimes pain is unavoidable. These skills help us cope with difficult emotions and experiences that are part of life, without making things worse.

The structure of this workbook maps out onto the common stages and experiences in the dating process, rather than going through the DBT skills sequentially or covering all the skills comprehensively. DBT skills are presented in ways they might help us navigate and cope with dating situations and scenarios. First, before meeting anyone or putting yourself out there, in Chapter 1, you will ground yourself in DBT's core skills to learn to listen and trust your own Wise Mind throughout the dating process. You will get clear on your intentions and what you are looking for in a partner before launching into the world of dating. You will set yourself up for stability by learning self-care strategies. Chapter 2 helps you to overcome any resistance and offers tools to quell the voices telling you that you are not ready or good enough to date. Chapter 3 will help you practice being mindful and present while communicating on dating apps, while meeting people in person, and on the date itself, and cover strategies to communicate effectively so you can better assess compatibility and assert your desires and needs. Chapter 4 is all about after the date, when thoughts and emotions tend to run wild and folks tend to ruminate, fixate, obsess, or are confused about how they feel about someone. Finally, Chapter 5 invites you to keep DBT skills front of mind to ensure a budding relationship is on the right track. I have done my best to include a variety of scenarios that friends, clients, or I, myself, have experienced. If I missed something, I hope the skills and examples will give you enough to work with so that you can apply them to your own life.

Dating *is* hard, but with the help of DBT skills, you've got this!

## PEP TALK

*Pause, breathe. Here is a Loving Little Pep Talk.*

For anyone who is looking for love online, on the apps, or in real life, I want to send out beams of strength and support your way. There will be moments when you want to give up, when you feel discouraged and lonely, when you start to question your worthiness or the sanity of a particular gender or the human race. There will be times when you look for fault in yourself and times when you blame the city you live in and start to think that all the wonderful people in your zip code must be taken.

Dating is a roller coaster of emotions for nearly everyone who approaches the process with the intention of genuine connection because there are so many others out there who have either different intentions or lack the skills to communicate their true feelings and goals. Dating apps also encourage superficial connection and offer the illusion of endless options.

As impossible as it may seem to find love, remember that **it only takes one person**. Even if 99 out of 100 people are self-absorbed, ghost you, or aren't your jam, (and I promise that the real odds are much more in your favor than 1/100) there is 1 person out there you will feel attracted to and enjoy spending time with and want to continue to get to know. That one person is all you need. Not "the one" but someone who can become the right one person for you, over time, with mutual effort.

Use the skills in this workbook to continually remind yourself of what values you hope to live out in a relationship and of what needs are the most important to you. You will find a like-minded quality person with values that complement your own. The less time you waste on the obvious mismatches and the clearer you are on your intentions and needs upfront, the sooner you will find someone with whom to build a loving partnership. I am here cheering you on every step of the way!

# CHAPTER ONE

## *Before You Date*

**Get to know Wise Mind.**

Mindfulness is at the core of the DBT curriculum. Mindfulness allows us to be fully present in our lives and aware of our moment-to-moment experiences without judgment of ourselves, our emotions, sensations, thoughts, and of life. Wise Mind is the fullest expression of that state—when we are compassionate, curious, calm, and open. When we are connected to Wise Mind, we are able to listen to and respond to life from our inner wisdom, so that we can make choices that are in alignment with our values and needs. You can imagine that letting Wise Mind lead you in the dating process can bring much more clarity, stability, and fulfillment than if you were to let your changing moods and impulses, or in contrast, your cool logic and task-oriented thinking to be in control.

Emotion mind is moody, hot, ruled by urges, impulses, and judgments. When we are in emotion mind, we experience our emotions as big and overpowering, and are often driven to acting before having the space to sort out fact from our interpretations. Rational mind is cool, detached, informed by logic, facts, and reason. In reasonable mind we solve problems and complete tasks but may overlook our needs and relational considerations. The goal of Wise Mind is not to rid ourselves of our emotions, nor to ignore pragmatics, but to integrate how we feel with what we know to be factually true and relevant. At this intersection, we follow our inner guidance and intuition. Wise Mind brings together emotion mind and rational mind to create something beyond both.

Emotions can offer us critical information about our needs and our priorities in life. Rational thinking is vital in making sound decisions based on an accurate view of life and the world. When we bring these together and drop into our *hut* (a term coined by Alexandra Franzen that combines heart + gut), we can tune into what feels like the next most authentic step we can take on our path.[3]

WISE MIND

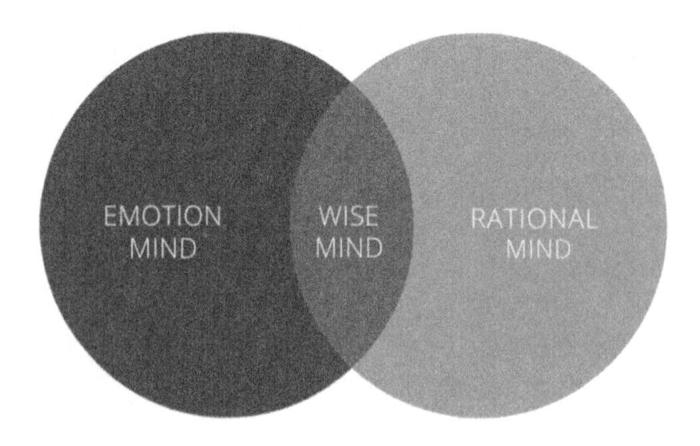


You might have experienced Wise Mind after practicing yoga asana, during a run, when feeling one with nature, or when at a crossroads and you've known without any doubts what was the right decision for you. Wise Mind can often be experienced in the body as a feeling of being centered and expansive. You might have the sense that you are stepping back from a situation to see it in its complexity with a feeling of peace and conviction. Take a moment now to float back to a time when you felt completely clear about a decision and could move forward with a sense of calm and ease.

Sometimes ease is not present, however, but we feel driven by what we know to be true and commit to action even though it is difficult or painful, because of that sense of truth. Can you think of a time when you had to follow your ethics because you were compelled by a sense of fairness or justice, and felt inner peace despite the outer chaos and pain? Take a moment to reflect and make notes on your experiences of Wise Mind.

What is an experience you have had of being in Wise Mind?

________________________________________________

________________________________________________

________________________________________________

________________________________________________

________________________________________________

________________________________________________

________________________________________________

When you are in Wise Mind, how do you feel in your body?

If you're having a difficult time recalling any experiences of Wise Mind, that's okay. Accessing Wise Mind can be tricky, and takes practice with paying attention, slowing down, and respecting our deepest needs. However, recognizing that we are not in Wise Mind can be just as helpful as accessing Wise Mind. When we can at least identify that we are in a state ruled by emotions, judgment, and urges, we can be careful to delay making important decisions right then, and to take a pause and wait for intense emotions to subside before taking the next step. If we are feeling disconnected from all emotion and can only think of what the most practical decision would be, we need to wait until we can tune into compassion for self and others.

What are some signs that you are not in Wise Mind—emotions, sensations, thoughts that tend to be present in either emotion mind or rational mind?

______________________________________________

______________________________________________

______________________________________________

______________________________________________

______________________________________________

______________________________________________

**Wise Mind Exercises.**

All of us have Wise Mind, though sometimes it can be challenging to tune in. Practice and notice which of these work for you. We will return to Wise Mind throughout the dating process to check in and make sure our decisions are driven by what is best for us. These are updated and adapted from the DBT Skills Training Handouts and Worksheets, 2nd Edition, by Marsha Linehan:[4]

1. Consider a question you want guidance around. Start simple, such as "How can I best take care of myself today?" or "What music would I most like to listen to now?" Close your eyes and allow your attention to drop into your slowing breath, the rise and fall of your chest and stomach. Ask the question to yourself and pause to allow a response to arise naturally, while tuning into your breath and body. If the answer comes from the mind and you are drawn into thoughts, this is not Wise Mind. Let an answer float into your awareness when quiet and attending to the breath. If this feels challenging, please know that is normal when we are just starting out with getting to know Wise Mind. Move onto another practice.

2. Visualize a serene lake in the woods on a breezy, sunny, pleasant day. Imagine that the sparkling blue green water makes gentle movements, lapping at the shore, where lush green grass grows and flowers bloom. You are a thin flake of stone that finds your way into the lake. You drop into the placid water and are drifting slowly, circling softly, downwards to the bottom of the lake. Sense the gentle descent. Notice that it is quiet and calming to swirl slowly down to the center of the lake. Notice the peace and feel the relaxing turns as you float down in the deep crystal blue waters. Feel how you safely land on the soft blanket of sand at the bottom and take in the calm and ease there. Absorb this feeling of settled quiet and open your eyes while maintaining awareness of that centeredness within you.

3. Find a comfortable position seated or lying down. Take a moment to release any tension that you notice in your jaw, your shoulders, neck, or back by adjusting and stretching. Breathe in and out at your own natural rhythm, drawing your attention to your breath as it fills and leaves your lungs. As you engage in mindful breathing, allow yourself to notice the pause after each inhale and each exhale. Notice the stillness within each pause. Allow yourself to find peace at the top of the breath and peace at the bottom of the breath. At a moment that feels natural, drop into the pause at the bottom of your breath and let it rest there for a few seconds, notice a settling and relaxation of your body. Resume the cycles of inhale and exhale and practice the pause at the bottom as it feels comfortable and easy. Sense the calmness and openness as you sink into your center at the bottom of your breath.

### Understanding Emotions

Has an emotion ever made you feel closer to someone or enhanced good experiences? Maybe you've felt overwhelmed with love for someone or an animal, felt moved by art or music, felt awe while taking in a landscape, or joy when laughing and connecting with friends. Neuroscientists understand that emotions developed as an evolutionary function—our feelings can move us towards people and environments that support our survival and allow us to thrive and help us remember and replicate experiences that have been positive and safe. Likewise, the distressing emotions we feel can alert us to threat, signal when there is a problem we need to solve or a situation we need to leave and can help protect us from repeating those experiences. For some of us, emotions come on quickly and intensely, and in our overwhelm, we can neglect to understand the information they convey. If we think of difficult emotions as something bad that we need to get rid of, this not only means we might miss the message in the emotion, but also add more suffering by going to battle against our emotions.

Emotion regulation skills can help us to approach our emotions with curiosity and acceptance, looking at our situations more objectively, and proceeding with Wise Mind to balance both feelings and facts. Breaking down our emotional responses into the smaller parts that contribute to our feelings can help make sense of our emotions and help us approach them with more understanding. There are many possible influences that shape the intensity and type of emotions we experience. DBT's "Model for Describing Emotions" presents several components to explain the psychological and biological process that creates our inner state:[5]

*Vulnerability factors and stressors* set us up to feel more intense and upsetting emotions. For instance, we are more susceptible to feeling sensitive when we are not rested, under a lot of stress, sick, aren't getting proper nutrition, or if we have a trauma history. Some are more likely to feel overwhelmed in crowds, or where there are loud sounds or other sensory stimuli. Some need sufficient alone time before they have energy to socialize and connect with others. We have some ability to help ourselves out by adjusting our daily routines, finding healthy outlets to release stress, or not putting ourselves in situations we know make us feel more vulnerable.

*Experiences and Events* themselves can be challenging. Conflict or tension at work or in our home environment and other stressful situations in our life can certainly contribute to having an emotional response. Events can be something external that happens, what someone else says or does, or an internal thought or our own behaviors. At times we are unable to change our environment but often we do have agency to make healthy decisions and to leave relationships, jobs, and situations that cause pain.

*Stories and beliefs* we tell ourselves about an event are often the cause of our emotions more than the event on its own. We tend to quickly interpret our experiences and some of us are more likely to view a neutral act through a negative lens and jump to catastrophic thoughts. What we tell ourselves about a situation may not be accurate but can feel true when the emotional response we have is strong. For instance, if someone doesn't text us back right away, we can spin out into our worst fears. We might jump to conclusions that someone dislikes us or start judging ourselves as unlovable or worthless. Distinguishing the facts from the stories we are telling ourselves can help reduce stressful feelings.

*Body and brain changes* are how we become aware that we are feeling something other than neutral. Biochemical reactions to stimuli in our environments and to our own thoughts happen in several brain systems and throughout the body, changing our heart rate, digestion, muscle tone, temperature, immune function, nervous system, and breathing. When we experience these sensations and biological shifts, we can recognize that this is an automatic process that is meant to get our attention to information about relative threat or safety. We can step back and assess whether our body is responding accurately to a current situation or if there might be a disconnect between the facts of the moment and our physical response. Intentionally changing the breath and other physiological interventions can help regulate the stress response and bring us back to a calmer state.

*Secondary Emotions* is the phenomenon of reacting to our initial emotional response. On top of the original distress we feel, we flood ourselves with self-invalidating thoughts, myths about emotions, or other judgmental interpretations of our feelings that cause more distress. Those who grew up having their feelings minimized, dismissed, or mocked, and those who were taught what they were feeling was "bad" or "wrong," often shame and judge themselves for having emotions. Learning to allow our emotions and accept difficult emotions as part of being human, can decrease our negative reactions to our feelings.

*Behaviors and expressions* are the external actions we take, words we say, and non-verbal cues we give to share our emotions. If we slow down and pause before acting, it will be less likely we do something impulsive that we later regret.

Use this understanding of emotion to gain insight into why you feel the way you do, and to remain aware of the biochemical and psychological reasons for your emotions rather than criticize yourself and your inner experience. As you start dating, stay mindful of what kinds of situations and connections promote more stability and calm, and which lead to more chaos, stress, or heightened or panicked states.

**Mindfulness of Emotions. What does a healthy relationship feel like?**

Many of you might have been told that you are "too sensitive," "too emotional," and that your feelings come across as intense. DBT does not ask us to dispense with our emotions. Instead, we want to transform our relationship with our emotions. Emotions are necessary because they communicate to ourselves and others our needs and can move us into action. When we are mindful, we are able to respond to our emotions without leading to distress, overwhelm, or impulsive actions.

When we learn to identify and understand our emotions, and have tools to process, release, or effectively express them, our sense of grounding and safety in the world increases. We can also make Wise Mind choices to pursue activities and relationships that reduce our vulnerability to painful emotions and improve our quality of life.

I think back to some of my relationships and remember how it felt when my needs for intimacy or support were made out to be unreasonable or when I was left on my own and offered no comfort in my most vulnerable and shaky moments. I felt excitement and passion in the beginning of those relationships, but over time that was replaced with doubts, fear, confusion, and loneliness.

In contrast, when I was in a relationship with someone who was reliable, treated me kindly, listened to my needs and did their best to meet them, while I also worked to attend to theirs, I felt a sense of calm, trust, ease, and relaxation. I felt content and warm inside.

Noticing how we feel in our relationship can provide cues to whether it is a healthy and fulfilling partnership, or if maybe we are tolerating inappropriate behaviors to hold onto someone we are scared of losing, or to chase the excitement and thrill we felt at the beginning of a relationship.

The following exercise can help you identify how you would like to feel when you are in a healthy and satisfying relationship, over time, not just in the beginning.

Look over the list of feeling words below. Circle or highlight the words that resonate with how you imagine you would feel in a healthy, loving, and mutual relationship. Feel free to add your own.

*Healthy Relationship Emotions*

Alive—you feel vibrant and open to life and new experiences in your relationship

Calm—there is a quality of feeling at peace and soothed in your relationship

Comfortable—you can be yourself with your partner and feel at ease

Confident—you feel sure of yourself and know that you matter and have a lot to offer

Centered—you are grounded and trust yourself to make good decisions

Excited—you look forward to spending time with your partner and achieving dreams together

Expansive—you have a sense of relaxation and trust in life and the future about your relationship

Free—you feel able to explore and grow as an individual even while in partnership

Grateful—you feel fulfilled and appreciative that this person is in your life

Grounded—you feel mindful and are secure in the connection to yourself and partner

Inspired—you feel connected to your creativity and moved to self-expression

Joyful—you experience laughter, delight, and openness together

Loved/Loving—you feel warmth and affection towards your partner and experience those in return

Motivated—the relationship encourages you to move towards your goals and you feel energized

Passionate—your relationship allows you to express desires and experience sensual excitement

Proud—you feel a sense of achievement and contentment in who you are and the life you've led

Safe—you feel secure and able to show up vulnerably in your relationship

Stimulated—you feel intellectually challenged and engaged

Strong—you feel capable, determined, and empowered in your body

Turned on—you are attracted to your partner and enjoy exploring and expressing your sexuality with them

Any you would add?

______________________________________________

______________________________________________

Think about how you want to feel, overall, in your relationship. Importantly, when we are with someone who fights fair, we should continue to know we are safe and loved even during disagreements. Conflict happens in all relationships and is a necessary part of deepening intimacy. If we are with someone who resorts to what Dr. Julie and John Gottman refer to as the *4 Horsemen*—criticism (attacking someone's character rather than expressing a complaint about a specific behavior); defensiveness (turning the blame back to the partner raising concerns and making excuses instead of taking responsibility); stonewalling (shutting down and withdrawing from an interaction by physically leaving or turning away and becoming unresponsive); or contempt (condescension, mocking, disrespect, or insults, putting your partner down)—as a regular pattern when trying to resolve issues, then eventually this will erode trust and security.[6] We are looking for the 5:1 ratio that the Gottmans identify in their research of successful couples. During a conflict, there should be 5 positive interactions for every 1 negative. While you or your partner may slip into a moment of stonewalling, criticism or defensiveness, there needs to be intentional use of humor, affection, apology, reflecting feelings, etc. to soften the tone of the interaction. (Contempt should never be present and is a clear warning sign in a relationship that calls for professional support).

This 5:1 ratio can help us feel safe and secure, even when in conflict with a partner. With that in mind, write a few sentences about how you would like to feel with your partner both in your best and most challenged moments.

_______________________________________________

_______________________________________________

_______________________________________________

_______________________________________________

_______________________________________________

_______________________________________________

_______________________________________________

Now note the words from the list below that describe how it might feel if you are in an unhealthy relationship. It will be important to practice mindfulness of emotions when you are on dates, communicating in between dates, as things progress with a partner, and when deciding whether to commit to or let go of a connection. Consider and highlight which feeling words could be a warning to you that things are off or unhealthy in a relationship.

*Troubled Relationship Emotions*

Addicted—you feel a sense of urgency and craving for contact when apart from your partner

Afraid—you feel on edge and worry about angering your partner

Anger—you experience intense feelings when things don't go your way or as you hoped they would

Annoyed—you feel impatient and upset around your partner or when thinking about them

Anxious—you worry about losing the relationship if you don't say or do the "right" thing or worry about losing yourself by getting too close to your partner

Appalled—you feel shocked at their behaviors towards you or others

Bored—you feel uninspired and disconnected with your partner

Confused—you feel ambivalence towards your partner or don't know the status of your relationship and wonder how your partner truly feels about you

Contempt—you are feeling resentful or starting to think negatively about who your partner is as a person

Disappointment—you feel hurt or letdown by your partner's actions or inaction

Disconcerted—you have concerns about your relationship and feel unsettled

Disoriented—sometimes you don't know what is real or not, you feel like you can't always trust your own version of events and feel lost during conversations or conflict with your partner

Dread—you feel apprehensive and experience negative anticipation before conversations or interactions with your partner

Guilt—you feel a sense of responsibility for your partner's well-being and worry you aren't doing enough for them

Exhausted—you feel tired from emotional ups and downs or from not taking proper care of your basic needs

Flooded—you feel overwhelmed with intense sensation or emotion

Inadequate—you worry that you are not "good enough" for your partner and feel less than

Insecure—you don't trust the relationship can endure conflict or worry that your partner may leave at any time

Isolated—you find yourself feeling alone and reluctant or unable to reach other to others outside your relationship

Jealous—you feel suspicious of your partner's other relationship or insecure about their past relationships

Lonely—you don't feel known or seen in your relationship and long for more intimacy

Sad—you experience hurt from not having needs met

Shame—you feel like there is something wrong with you that is causing the issues in your relationship, or believe that if you left there would be no one else to love you

Stressed—you find you are in *fight, flight, or freeze* a lot in your relationship

You may need to discern whether your uncomfortable emotions are due to your relationship, or other factors in your life or unresolved issues from your past, creeping into the present. And, if you are noticing some of these feelings of jealousy, contempt, anger coming out towards your partner, a first step would be to take responsibility for your part in the dynamic, and then to meet with a couple's therapist to work on improving your relationship.

If you consistently are feeling more of the emotions from this lower list compared to the one above, something needs to be changed, and seeking out support from a psychologist or psychotherapist is recommended.

Reflect on which list of words most resonates with you now, as someone who is unpartnered. It's normal to feel sad, lonely, and experience stress in our life at times. And it is also a myth that you need to be fulfilled on your own before getting into a relationship—it's okay if you are someone who prefers the companionship of being partnered. However, you are more likely to thrive in your next relationship if you do attend to problem solving the situations in your life that cause unnecessary stress or pain, and if you have some strategies to reduce or cope with difficult emotions.

Consider where in your life you can choose to set boundaries, try new activities, practice self-care, or work to reduce negative self-talk to generate more positive emotions:

________________________________________

________________________________________

________________________________________

________________________________________

________________________________________

________________________________________

________________________________________

**Naming your Needs**

It can be helpful to incorporate an awareness of needs into our understanding of emotions. We enter romantic relationships in part to meet a variety of our social, emotional, physical, and intellectual needs. Since it is not possible for one person to meet all our needs, some will necessarily be met by friends, family, our professional lives, and our extended communities. If you practice polyamory or consensual non-monogamy, you are familiar with this and are likely already thinking about what kinds of new connections you are wanting in your life to feel fulfilled. Even in monogamous relationships, placing the pressure on one partner to meet all needs will lead to disappointment or codependency. All of us can reflect, then, on which of our needs *must* be met in our next romantic relationship.

While this naming of our needs is not a part of the DBT curriculum and is informed, rather, by Non-Violent Communication (NVC), I include it because it can provide us with key information.[7]

The presence of an emotion often signals that some of our needs are either being met or unmet. For example, I have felt content and safe in a relationship when my needs for consideration and support are met. Alternately, I have felt agitated and addicted when my needs for consistent communication and closeness have not been met. Here is another example. If you are consistently feeling joyful with someone because they meet your needs for humor and play, but then you feel frustrated and confused by unmet needs for emotional or sexual intimacy, you can evaluate how you feel in the context of which needs are most crucial or non-negotiable for you. If you know that you can have your need for play and humor met in other relationships but having sexual and emotional closeness in your partnership is a necessary, then there is now clarity that this person may make a great friend, but not a great romantic partner for you.

Of course, it could be worth having a conversation about needs before just giving up on a connection, to see if more attention to those needs can make a shift in the dynamic. Either way, this can provide you with meaningful insight into your relationships—what is and isn't working and why.

Look over the following vocabulary of needs and make a note of 5-7 that are most vital in your romantic partnerships.

ACCEPTANCE, AFFECTION, APPRECIATION, BELONGING, COOPERATION, COMMUNICATION, CLOSENESS, COMMUNITY, COMPANIONSHIP, COMPASSION, CONNECTION, CONSIDERATION, CONSISTENCY, EMPATHY, INCLUSION, INTIMACY, LOVE, NURTURING, RESPECT, SAFETY, SECURITY, SEXUAL INTIMACY, STABILITY, SUPPORT, TO KNOW AND BE KNOWN, TO SEE AND BE SEEN, TO UNDERSTAND AND BE UNDERSTOOD, TRUST, WARMTH, HONESTY, AUTHENTICITY, INTEGRITY, PRESENCE, PLAY, JOY, HUMOR, EQUALITY, FAIRNESS, MUTUALITY, HARMONY, INSPIRATION, ORDER, CHOICE, FREEDOM, INDEPENDENCE, SPACE, SPONTANEITY, CHALLENGE, CLARITY, COMPETENCE, CONTRIBUTION, CREATIVITY, EFFICACY, GROWTH, HOPE, LEARNING, PARTICIPATION, PURPOSE, SELF-EXPRESSION, TO MATTER

Jot down your thoughts about your past relationship experiences—identify some of the predominant emotions you felt and the needs you had that were either met or unmet. What are your thoughts and feelings now as you reflect on those previous experiences?

______________________________________________

______________________________________________

______________________________________________

______________________________________________

______________________________________________

______________________________________________

Summarize in a few sentences what you are looking for in your next relationship in terms of priority needs and emotions you would like to feel with your significant other.

______________________________________________

______________________________________________

______________________________________________

______________________________________________

______________________________________________

Do you have any patterns of neglecting your own needs?

What are some ways you can attend to your needs through changing your self-talk, building more support networks, or setting boundaries that may help bring you more fulfillment before jumping into the dating pool?

**Attachment needs—balancing intimacy and independence**

Attachment Theory describes the ways we bond and look for a sense of safety in relationships. Attachment theory is based on studies first conducted with parents and infants in the 1970s. Researchers found that children responded in a few types of patterned ways when separated from then reunited with their primary caregiver. Psychologists have categorized these distinct reactions into the attachment styles that we often see emerge as adults when we pair bond. The table below describes the 4 types that psychologists have identified.

| Secure | Anxious-Ambivalent | Dismissive-Avoidant | Fearful-Avoidant |
|---|---|---|---|
| Attachment needs mostly met in childhood, as child felt loved despite moods or behaviors. Caregivers set aside own emotions to focus on child's developmental needs. | Parents often made child feel responsible for the adults' emotions, had co-dependent relationship with child, did not teach child how to self-soothe or problem solve. Parental attention or affection could be unpredictable, hot/cold. | Parents were often not emotionally available, distant, neglectful, critical. Little physical affection given, overly strict, or discouraged dependency upon parents to meet needs, even when age appropriate to be dependent. | Oftentimes, the child experienced trauma in childhood and experienced caregiver as threatening or unsafe. Parent often had own unresolved trauma that led to chaotic, confusing, and conflicting moods and behaviors. |

| Secure | Anxious-Ambivalent | Dismissive-Avoidant | Fearful-Avoidant |
|---|---|---|---|
| Enjoy intimacy, affection, and emotional connection | Enjoy intimacy, affection, and are emotionally expressive and giving. | Desire some closeness but have a threshold. Intimacy can feel threatening to their autonomy. Difficulty identifying or expressing emotions and needs. | Desire intimacy but are unable to fully trust that their partner is safe. As intimacy grows, fear often intensifies. |
| Enjoy their independence and alone time. | Fear abandonment and look for signs that they are or aren't loved in subtle shifts in mood, nonverbal cues, can be hypervigilant to detect threat of rejection. Can resort to anger or demands to elicit response they want from partner. | Value their sense of autonomy and self-sufficiency and are comfortable on their own, can readily problem solve. Often highly focused and high achieving. | Often experience a blend of attachment anxiety and avoidance, so at times feel relief in their alone time and other times crave closeness and can share vulnerably. Seem to move between hypervigilant and numbed out. |

| Secure | Anxious-Ambivalent | Dismissive-Avoidant | Fearful-Avoidant |
|---|---|---|---|
| Feel comfortable relying on others to meet their needs | Commit quickly to a partner and overfocus on the partner, neglect themselves to hold onto the relationship | Often avoid feeling dependent on others. Can view having needs as a weakness. Retreat when stressed. Resist feeling responsible for others' well-being through distancing. | Move between poles of distance/ self-reliance versus connection/ closeness with other. Often seek out support but don't fully trust it. |
| Can regulate emotions & resolve conflict constructively. Collaborate to come to resolutions. | Have difficulty regulating a sense of safety within themselves or managing emotions. Often need others to validate their experience before they trust themselves. | Often become flooded and overwhelmed during conflict and retreat, shutdown, or stonewall to cope. | Have difficulty regulating a sense of safety within themselves or managing emotions, which can present as lashing out, expressing contempt, or shutting down. |
| Easily cope with goodbyes and reunions with partner. | Do well with reunions but struggle with goodbyes | Do well with goodbyes and can struggle to reconnect. | Present with erratic and confusing behaviors that sometimes move towards connection and other times away. |

Another way to understand these 4 attachment types—

Those who are *Secure* feel safe both in relationship, with intimacy and on their own, are generally able to self-regulate and work constructively through conflict and enjoy relying on others and having others rely on them.

Those who lean *Anxious-Ambivalent* seek safety through strategies of increasing intimacy, closeness, or reassurance to avoid abandonment, rejection, and feelings of being unlovable.

Those who lean *Dismissive-Avoidant* seek safety through strategies of distancing and deactivation to avoid being controlled, losing their sense of self and freedom.

Those who lean *Fearful-Avoidant* seek safety through a mix of growing intimacy and distancing, to balance out fears of rejection, inadequacy, and loss of self.

As you review these attachment styles and find resonance in any of the descriptions, resist the temptation to overidentify with or label yourself as this type in a totalizing way. It is currently very on trend, especially on social media, to center attachment styles above all else in the relationship and dating world. Like any other framework, it can offer some insight into our patterns, but it does not explain all behaviors and can be a very reductive lens through which to view human complexity. In my own work with clients, I have seen many who express these various traits on a spectrum depending on the type of relationship they're in and what specific attachment experiences they are having. Many people can show up as secure much of the time but have some insecure responses when a dynamic activates an old memory of insecurity.

If we know that we lean anxious, we may need to take responsibility for our emotions and not put them on our partner nor expect constant reassurance from them. If we show up as avoidant and resort to deactivating strategies to move away from intimacy, we may need to challenge ourselves to sit with the discomfort of closeness. Don't take these labels too far. It does not help us to judge ourselves and our partners as insecurely attached. Most humans will have moments of insecurity, and some behaviors will elicit an insecure response even in someone who leans secure. We can also learn to notice the attachment response without acting on it. Plenty of anxiously attached folks develop their Emotion Regulation skills so they don't put their fears onto their partners and plenty of avoidantly attached folks utilize Distress Tolerance skills to learn to stay put to work through challenges when they feel the urge to run.

When everything is attributed to attachment style, it can lead to people avoiding responsibility for their actions or distorting and dismissing their partner's reasonable responses as an insecure attachment behavior. For instance, when I spoke up about my former partner breaking promises and attempted to hold him accountable to his word, this was not anxiously attached "protest" behavior as he claimed, but rather, a natural response to a partner not keeping a commitment. Likewise, he would minimize the situation by claiming I was unfairly reacting to his valid avoidant behaviors. We can be sympathetic to avoidant urges like wanting to retreat and protect independence with more space, but in healthy adult relationships, these needs should be communicated explicitly to negotiate a way to build emotional safety. However, lying, not being transparent, and not following through on one's word are not traits of being avoidantly attached, but just unkind and self-centered behaviors.

Healthy communication involves expressing our hurts and disappointments when someone is not showing up consistently or is not being considerate. Interpersonal Effectiveness skills will be an important tool in building safety while negotiating needs. Two people who have insecure attachment can have a secure relationship through open conversation in which both people can share how they feel, what they need, and make requests that are fair and consider both of their experiences. Don't let someone tell you you're being "anxious" if you are raising a concern about connection in the relationship nor that you are "avoidant" if you request space. Also, don't excuse poor behavior by blaming it on an attachment wound. Our attachment styles do not cause us to treat people poorly.

Being aware of attachment can help in this sense: we all have parts of ourselves that experienced feeling unsafe in past relationships –whether parent-child, friendship, romantic, etc. These parts can get activated in the present and make us re-experience a past attachment threat or injury, or even an attachment hope or elation (as in "maybe this time I will be fully seen and loved). We can be mindful that we are making decisions about our relationships not from those wounded, fearful, or grasping parts, but from our Wise Mind. To review, Wise Mind is the calm, whole, truest version of ourselves that can witness those parts with compassion, without allowing them to drive our choices and behaviors. Knowing the ways that you can help restore a sense of safety in your nervous system, through self-soothing and other coping and mindfulness strategies, can help you to respond from the present, from Wise Mind, rather than from this past injury.

This is also why slowing down the dating process can be so helpful. In a rush of emotion, we can think we are feeling certainty and compatibility when it may be an adrenaline and fear response masking as bliss and excitement. It is natural to feel excitement about someone we feel attracted and drawn to. First make sure you are grounded in yourself, and in what is in your best interest for your emotional health and wholeness. When attachment fears kick up, practice noticing them, asking how you can show up for those parts of you, rather than use a connection with someone else to soothe them.

We all need a balance of closeness and autonomy in a healthy relationship, and rather than obsess about avoidant or anxious traits, try instead to tune into what will help you to feel secure and safe within yourself, even when someone else is not showing up the way you would like. Have upfront conversation about the ways you feel safe and the degree of closeness and distance that helps you feel relaxed and trusting. Work to communicate what needs you have that will help you feel more secure, and if someone is unwilling or unable to meet you there and you cannot reach a compromise, accept their answer, and move on. A lot of trouble comes from trying to force a connection to work when it clearly does not.

What are the cues that you are in an anxious, avoidant, or otherwise wounded part and may need to pause and regroup before acting or making relationship decisions? What signs are there that you are off center and out of Wise Mind?

________________________________________

________________________________________

________________________________________

________________________________________

________________________________________

________________________________________

________________________________________

________________________________________

*for example: I start to ruminate and worry about what someone is thinking about me, I try to do or say things that will keep them interested.*

How can you soothe your old attachment injuries and take care of the parts of you that look for safety outside yourself? How can you build a sense of inner security regardless of what is happening in your relationships?

_______________________________________________

_______________________________________________

_______________________________________________

_______________________________________________

_______________________________________________

_______________________________________________

_______________________________________________

_______________________________________________

*for example: I can validate the part of me that wants to be loved everyone wants this, but being inauthentic is counter to my goal, since then the person would be loving someone who I am pretending to be.*

**Using Long-Term Positives to build a relationship that supports your dreams and nurtures your values**

DBT teaches us that a powerful way to regulate our emotions is to live a life of meaning and purpose. We can reduce suffering and improve our mood by getting on a path that reflects our personal sense of ethics and priorities. Understanding our values can help us feel good about who we are and how we show up in our lives.

As you make connections and consider potential partners it will be important to assess their compatibility with your values and priorities in life. This exercise asks you to identify the principles that guide the direction you take in your life. While emotions describe our moment-to-moment internal experience, values and priorities are focused on the kind of person we would like to be. Core values reflect how we live out our own personal code of ethics. When you set goals based on your most cherished values, you are building a life of authenticity and fulfillment. Keeping these in mind when you date will help you find a partner who shares similar or compatible values. As you get to know someone, pay attention to how much they support and nurture your values even if they differ. Do they bring out the best qualities in you that reflect your ideals and aspirations? Are their behaviors and actions consistent with the values they profess?

I once was in a relationship in which I felt very special for receiving attention from my partner and was excited that someone I looked up to wanted to be with me. During most of our time together, I was on edge, irritable with others, withdrawn from friendships, and became petty and cynical. The longer I stayed with the person, the more those traits took over and the more I strayed from my core values.

If I had stepped back from the relationship to evaluate it, I would have seen I was not prioritizing the things I believe are most important. I did not assert healthy boundaries and compromised who I was so that I could feel connected to them. Rather than showing up as a distinct, whole person who stood up for what I believed in, I allowed myself to merge and become codependent with them and mirrored a lot of their personality. I was distraught when their contempt suddenly turned against me, and thankfully, had the strength to leave the relationship. As distraught as I was by the rejection, I noticed in the aftermath that there was a healing experience, as I returned to what I value and made amends with the people I had hurt by who I allowed myself to become during that time. As I recommitted myself to my values and my friendships, I remembered what true care and support felt like. It can be seductive when we feel good around someone who gives us positive attention, especially when they complain about and criticize others. This often makes us feel uniquely chosen as "good enough" to be with such a person. I wish I had held myself more accountable to my values, and noticed that excitement and connection with this person came at too high a cost to who I want to be in the world.

In contrast, when I was in a relationship with a veteran of the Peace Corps who actively volunteered in the community, this both encouraged me to participate more in contributing to society, giving back and made me feel appreciated for my strengths of caring, compassion, and generosity. In other words, these two distinct experiences illustrate how a relationship can bring out the worst or the best in us.

Read through the list and examples of values and select 3-5 that are most important to you from the list.[10]

Be careful to not answer in the way you think you "should." If no one knew what you selected, and no one would judge you, what would be your top priorities? Give yourself permission to be honest. Feel free to add another value if you don't see it in the list.

Return to this as a compass throughout the dating process, to make sure you are on track and that the people you are spending time with have values that you respect and are compatible with your own.

**Values**

Connection—have close and satisfying friendships, feel a sense of belonging, give and receive affection and love, have and keep close friends, spend time with family members, have people with whom to do activities, show up as a present and engaged friend, partner, family member, etc., be receptive to feedback and work through challenges that arise in relationships, spend quality time with people I care about, end destructive relationships

Leadership— have authority over systems or an organization, manage and lead people, decide how resources are used, be respected by others, be seen as successful and obtain recognition, be competitive with others

Creativity—use the arts to express the inner self, learn, practice, and hone a creative talent, view the world through a lens of art and poetry, innovate and use the imagination, engage the senses

Goal-oriented— achieve significant goals, be involved in important projects, be productive, work hard, be ambitious, keep growing and improving in life

Pleasure— have an enjoyable time, seek fun activities and things that offer satisfaction, have ample free time, enjoy my work, relax and vacation

Adventure— try new and different things in life, be daring seek out exciting events relationships and things, enjoy high-sensation activities, travel and explore

Tradition— practice humility and modesty, follow traditions and customs, respect authority and follow rules, treat others well, follow through on responsibilities and obligations

Autonomy— follow my own path in life, be self-directed, make my own decisions and feel free, be independent, take care of myself and those I'm responsible for, have freedom of thought and action, act in terms of my own priorities

Spirituality— live life according to spiritual principles, practice a faith or religion, gain an understanding of myself and my life's spiritual purpose, understand and do the will of God or higher consciousness and find spiritual or divine meaning in life

Stability— live in secure and safe environment, basically healthy and fit, prioritize mental health and wellness, have a steady income that meets my own and my family's needs

Compassion— be fair, treat people equally and provide equal opportunities, understand different people, be open minded, care for nature and the environment, be a steward of the land, consider others

Service— help people or animals in need, care for others' well-being and improve society, be committed to a cause or to a group that has a larger purpose beyond my own, donate time or money or effort, be committed to a group that shares my beliefs and values, find a calling that is in service to a higher good or well-being of a community

Personal growth— self-development, adhere to a personal philosophy of life, learn and do challenging things that help me grow and mature as a human, get out of my comfort zone, and test limits, exercise a growth mindset and be willing to struggle to learn new things

Integrity—acknowledge and stand up for my personal beliefs, be an honest and responsible person and keep my word to others, be courageous in facing and living life, be a person who pays debts to others and repairs damage I've caused, be accepting of myself, others, and life as it is, live without resentment, be willing to do the right thing even when it is hard

Other—is there something missing from this list that would better capture your values and orientation in life? Jot down some keywords here to describe it:

____________________________________________

____________________________________________

____________________________________________

____________________________________________

Write your thoughts about your top values and priorities in life and how this might be shared with a romantic partner. What kinds of activities do you imagine doing together and apart while in relationship so that you are living a life consistent with what you believe to be most important? How might a partner encourage and support you in being true to your values?

What made it easy or hard in your past relationships to live in alignment with your values?

How can you show up as a partner in a way that reflects your values and life priorities in your next relationship? Are there any changes you would like to make now in your life to be more in accordance with your values?

______________________________________________

______________________________________________

______________________________________________

______________________________________________

______________________________________________

______________________________________________

Check in with Wise Mind. What from this exercise is important to keep in mind during the highs and lows of dating?

______________________________________________

______________________________________________

______________________________________________

______________________________________________

**Self-care for emotional stability**

According to the biopsychosocial theory, humans are shaped both by their genetics and biochemistry, their personality, as well as their social environment. Oftentimes, those of us who come into the world with high sensitivity to stimuli and outside stressors grow up in environments that invalidate or dismiss our feelings, rather than teach us how to manage, cope, and problem solve. The more we have big emotional reactions to our environments and are chastised for having them without receiving guidance on how to self-soothe or cope, the more dysregulated we can become. As adults, we can find that our emotions often come on intensely and out-of-the-blue, and we can have a tough time recovering back to baseline. In times of relational frustrations and dating disappointments, emotion regulation skills are essential to keep us feeling safe and connected to our needs, rather than reacting from fear, anger, insecurity, or other painful emotions.

In identifying how you want to feel in relationship and what your values and priorities are in life, you've already taken a huge step towards building emotional resilience. When we reduce our negative life circumstances and replace them with activities, people, and experiences that reflect our values and meet our needs, our positive emotions increase.

11

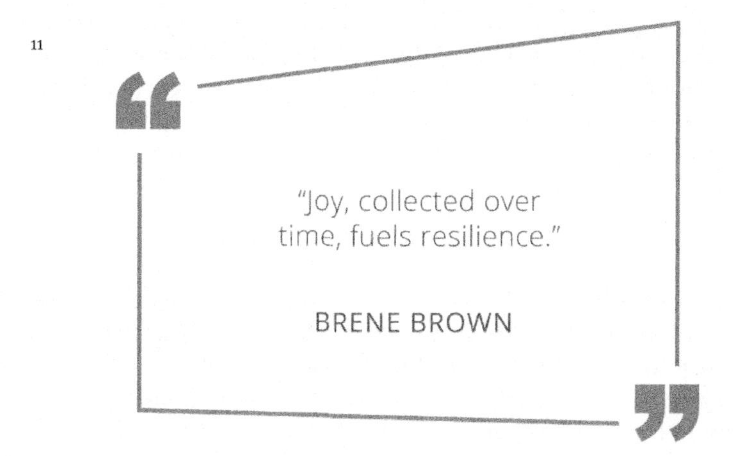

**PLEASE take care of your health and well-being while dating**

Planning a life centered around our ethics and mindful of our needs is one way to improve our emotional well-being, but it can take longer to experience the results of those efforts. Emotion regulation can also happen in the here-and-now. When we choose activities and environments that support our physical and psychological health and stability, we are reducing our vulnerability to big emotional swings, and increasing our ability to bounce back from stress.

To help regulate your emotions, make sure to tend to your basic needs. The risk and rejection experiences that are part of dating can leave us with a vulnerability hangover. The *PLEASE* skills in DBT are meant to help us to reduce vulnerability and promote emotion regulation. When you are taking care of your physical well-being, it will positively impact your mental and emotional health. This can set us up to be more resilient and less susceptible to extremes in thinking and emotional responses. Attending to the following can help you cope more effectively with the ups and downs of dating.

Please note, I have offered my own spin on the PLEASE skills and so this will differ from what you will find elsewhere in DBT literature.

Physical health—take medications as prescribed, treat illness, be proactive about going to medical appointments and checkups, do what you need to feel healthy and release tension in the body whether through massage therapy, acupuncture, masturbation, etc. When our physical health feels off, often our mental health is compromised, as well.

Light in the morning. I learned about the importance of daily sunlight from Dr. Huberman's neuroscience podcast and so I include it in my version of PLEASE. Research suggests that getting natural light every morning for at least 10 minutes can improve sleep, focus, and alertness.[12] This could be journaling or having coffee on your front porch, taking your dog for a walk, watering your plants outside—it does have to be outside. Don't stare at the sun, just be outside for about 10 minutes (double it on an overcast day) and this will help release cortisol in your brain required to feel awake for the day and regulate your circadian rhythm as well as your metabolism.

Eat nutritious and delicious foods that make you feel good. Be careful of restrictive eating and diets which can lead to disordered eating, avoid distorted ideals and beauty standards as well as social media comparisons that erode self-esteem. At the same time, when you can, avoid processed foods that are stripped of nutrients, and get your fill of fresh fruits and veggies. Notice when you are hungry and allow yourself to eat and enjoy your food.

Avoid substances that disrupt sleep or alter your mood or increase anxiety. Alcohol, caffeine, and other drugs can be disruptive to sleep, as well as change our brain chemistry, which affects our emotions. Many find that occasional marijuana use reduces anxiety or helps them sleep, while others will experience increased paranoia, anxiety, or brain fog. If you have had a habit of using any substance, whether caffeine, weed, or alcohol, it may be informative to stop use for a couple weeks, and then reintroduce slowly, tracking moods and energy levels, to get a good grasp on how it is impacting you. Recent research has shown that hallucinogens like psilocybin or MDMA can be therapeutic, but access to these therapy programs is still limited, and exercising caution with psychedelics is wise when you have a history of emotion dysregulation.

Sleep 7-9 hours a night. Insufficient sleep can make us more sensitive to life's stressors and cause long-term health problems, and too much sleep can hijack our energy levels and is linked with headaches, depression, and other health complications. Balancing sleep hugely helps our mental well-being. Establish a nightly routine to wind down. Avoid light, including screens, from about 10pm-4am.

Exert yourself or move for fun each day. Exercise does not have to be grueling and intense. You can put on an upbeat song and dance and bop around, take a walk while listening to a podcast, follow along with a fun online class, do some Jazzercise or a fun fitness program like NIA, go swimming in a local river, chase some Pokémon or walk your dog around the block.

Rate how you are doing on each of the PLEASE skills on a scale of 1-10, 10 being the best and 1 being needs the most work. Jot down ideas about how you will give that area of wellness some attention if needed.

________________________________________

________________________________________

________________________________________

________________________________________

________________________________________

________________________________________

________________________________________

________________________________________

**Reality Acceptance: get ready for emotional ups, downs, and sideways feelings**

From my work as a psychotherapist, as a friend to fellow singles, and from my own personal life, I know all too well how maddening and confusing dating can feel these days. The DBT antidote to facing disruptive and disorienting conditions that are outside of our control is Radical Acceptance, from the Distress Tolerance module. Just like it sounds, Distress Tolerance skills teach us to tolerate the difficulties of life, and the difficult emotions that come with those experiences.

*Radical Acceptance* or *Reality Acceptance* is the heart of the Distress Tolerance module. This skill can help us to move forward despite the problems and potential risks inherent to swiping and searching for a compatible mate. This approach is focused on allowing our experiences to be just as they are, as shitty as they are, without fixating on thoughts that things should be different than how they are.

The idea behind this mindset is that we can reduce unnecessary suffering by being with our experience and processing it, rather than adding to the already painful experiences of life with protests and complaints about the fact that what is happening should not be happening. This doesn't mean we can't feel angry or upset when we are treated poorly or when someone doesn't reciprocate our feelings. Rather, we work to accept those feelings, as much as we accept that those hurts are part of life, and part of courtship. This skill assumes that all humans sometimes experience distress, that it cannot always be avoided, but that we can learn how to cope effectively, and get back up after a fall.

*Radical Acceptance* will come in handy when you're trying your best to cope with annoyances and stings that come with the dating territory. Here the word "acceptance" does not mean like or approve of. It simply means we fully acknowledge and no longer fight reality as it is. You can start practicing Radical

Acceptance by facing this fact: dating will have its frustrations and disappointments, hurt feelings and bruised egos. Believing that it "should" be easy, smooth sailing or arguing that people "should" behave respectfully or rationally is understandable, but it is not being realistic. As much as you can, try to depersonalize the experience of dating. Dating is annoying for nearly everyone, and most who put in any effort at all will find they're doing most of the work in trying to connect with little coming back. Please know that dating comes with these challenges and if it feels exhausting, that is because a lot of the time it is!

With the Radical Acceptance skill, we work to stop fighting the reality. Instead of feeling surprised and upset each time one of the garden variety frustrations of dating occurs, we can learn to take it in stride, with self-talk that reminds us that these experiences are normal but that we are equipped to deal with them without taking them personally. Radical Acceptance is an ongoing process, not a one and done exercise.

Here are some ways to practice.[13]

Each time any frustration, exhaustion, discouraging feelings come, first notice, name, and then validate.

Make space for these feelings and remind yourself that these are common and understandable to feel while dating, that you are not alone, and you will get through it.

Observe and allow the sensations and emotions that come up as you work towards acceptance.

Do not judge any emotion or thought and give yourself permission to have the experience you are having. Notice the urge to judge, avoid, or get rid of an emotion, and instead relax around the sensations and energy in your body or say out loud, "I am feeling ___________ and that is okay. It is normal to have these feelings. Dating is hard."

Remember that behaviors like ghosting, lack of effort, poor communication, etc. that you are encountering *are not a reflection of you*, but of skills others are lacking. You can name out loud or write down those facts as well, "Sometimes people are not thoughtful, lack skills, or are rude and unkind. That is a part of life. I know I must accept this and cannot change the facts. It is okay to feel hurt and disappointed by the behavior. I believe I will find someone more open, kind, and skillful if I keep at it."

**Distract skillfully**

If you find yourself so anxious or agitated about some of your experiences that you can't practice Radical Acceptance yet, you can try another Distress Tolerance skill: *Distract.* Yes, in DBT Distract can be a skill. While distracting all the time would lead to problematic avoidance, sometimes it can be wise to distract if we just need to get through a temporary uncomfortable feeling and don't feel like we can change our emotions through developing new thoughts or behaviors.

You can distract through enjoyable activities, engaging the senses, or eliciting different emotions through music, tv, or movies that pull you away from the difficult feelings. Distract with any activity, whether useful like cleaning, planning a trip, or cooking or recreational like videogames, tv, masturbating, or coloring. Activities that engage the mind like crossword puzzles and brain games can shift our attention from anxious thoughts. Watching stand-up comedy or a horror film can create new emotions that help us focus less on the unpleasant emotions related to our own situation. And contributing to others through volunteering or focusing on those in need of support can offer a break from our own worries.

In DBT we use the acronym, *ACCEPTS*, to make it easier to remember:[14]

Activities that move your attention to something positive, relaxing, or engaging.

Contribute to friends, loved ones, or your community to shift focus off own problems and feel rewarded by helping someone else.

Comparison to others who are suffering, which is meant to help us appreciate that we may have things to feel thankful for even when things are hard, but many clients find this invalidating. When I teach DBT, I change this "C" to Compassion for others who are also suffering. When we imagine ourselves united in a shared experience of the human condition, we may not feel so alone. Breathe in for all beings in pain, breathe out compassion for everyone, yourself included. Or we can look at how we have grown or made progress compared to an earlier time in our own lives.

Emotions refers to choosing to interact with music, film, tv, or art that evokes strong emotions that are different than the distressing feelings you're experiencing. Watching a scary horror film, watching your favorite sitcom, listening to an uplifting playlist can pull you out of your mood through creating other emotions.

Pushing away means we visualize putting the situation we are upset about away for the time being. Try to picture placing your problem in a container, on a shelf, in a spaceship and sending it away, whatever works for you. This is an imaginal exercise designed to give you a break from ruminating on something upsetting.

Thoughts that are engaging and involve interesting problem solving or cognitive exercises pull the brain away from distress. This could be number or word puzzles, listing state capitals or naming all the places you'd like to travel to, reciting lyrics to a song.

Sensations can bring us into the present and offer an immersive experience to shift us out of distress. Engage the five senses.

Some ideas: squeeze a stress ball, use a fidget toy, take a hot or cold shower, have some mint tea, eat sour candy or spicy food.

Using the ACCEPTS skill, make a list of ideas you can turn to for positive distraction from stressful thoughts:

_______________________________________________

_______________________________________________

_______________________________________________

_______________________________________________

_______________________________________________

_______________________________________________

_______________________________________________

**Self-soothing**

*Self-soothe* is another Distress Tolerance skill we can use to cope when we are in emotion mind and are finding it hard to shift into Wise Mind, practice Radical Acceptance, or change our thoughts and behaviors.

This skill involves using touch, taste, sight, sound, or smells to help downshift our bodies and emotions towards a state of safety.

Find the tools that help to calm your nervous system. Look at the following checklist of ideas and select the self-soothing options that appeal most to you:

- ☐ Prepare a fragrant hot tea and slowly sip while inhaling the aroma.
- ☐ Eat a favorite food, savoring the taste of each bite.
- ☐ Settle into a comfortable chair and use a heating pad or weighted blanket.
- ☐ Take a nature walk and notice the beauty around you or be mindful of nature sounds.
- ☐ Light a scented candle and take in the scent or focus on the flickering of the flame.
- ☐ Cuddle with your pet and put your attention onto the sensations of touch.
- ☐ Hold an object that has significance to you or that feels smooth, heavy, or comforting to the touch. Focus on how this object feels in your hand.
- ☐ Blast some upbeat and invigorating music or play soft and soothing music and notice the sounds and shifts in energy.
- ☐ Watch a nature documentary.
- ☐ Do legs-up-the-wall pose by laying on the floor as you scoot up to a wall and rest your legs against the wall, so they are fully supported.
- ☐ Sing or hum.
- ☐ Use aromatherapy: find sharp scents to feel more alert or pleasant or relaxing scents for calm.
- ☐ Buy fresh flowers and notice the colors and shapes, take in the fragrance.
- ☐ Take a drive with favorite music and windows rolled down to feel the breeze on your arm or face.
- ☐ Get a professional massage.
- ☐ Take an Epsom salt bath and notice the sensation of the water on skin and the scent of the salts.
- ☐ Look at an artist's work that you enjoy.
- ☐ Notice the sounds, smells, sights where you are now, take these in slowly.

- ☐ Put on comfortable clothing or wrap yourself in a cozy blanket.
- ☐ Listen to ocean sounds.
- ☐ Place one hand on your chest and one on your belly and notice as they rise and fall with each belly breath.
- ☐ Take a shower and then massage a favorite lotion or oil onto your skin.
- ☐ Add some of your own ideas below:

______________________________

______________________________

______________________________

______________________________

**Wise Mind Check in**

Take a moment now to do a Wise Mind check in. When you get quiet and tune into your intuition, what are some insights you will take away from the previous exercises? What feels most true or important to keep in mind at this stage in your dating journey?

______________________________

______________________________

______________________________

______________________________

CHAPTER TWO

# *If you're Delaying Dating*

## Avoid avoiding

Do you find yourself procrastinating on putting up your profile on a dating app? Or ignoring messages in your inbox or delaying meeting a match in person?

If you are longing for a relationship but are delaying getting into the dating pool or scheduling dates to meet people, you're not alone. It can be overwhelming, intimidating, exhausting, especially if you've been out there for a while and nothing has seemed to stick. Many things that are worthwhile will involve some amount of risk and vulnerability. Author Alain de Botton declares in his *New York Times* essay, "Why you will marry the wrong person:"

> Choosing whom to commit ourselves to is merely a case of identifying which particular variety of suffering we would most like to sacrifice ourselves for," because, he explains, "every human will frustrate, anger, annoy, madden and disappoint us — and we will (without any malice) do the same to them.[15]

The reality of all relationships is that there will be hurt feelings and trying times but working through these with someone we trust, and love can be a rewarding process if it deepens our connection and understanding of each other.

The urge to self-protect is understandable. Yet closing ourselves off and retreating guarantees that we will not meet our goals and may miss out on a fulfilling connection. Even if there is pain along the way, we feel most rewarded when we move through and face our fears. Then we discover that we were stronger than we thought and realize that we can build a secure long-term relationship based on care and the willingness to repair and learn when we stumble.

Risking rejection and getting close to someone can be scary. If it helps to think of a time when you were able to overcome something challenging or you put yourself out there even though you were scared, please draw on that memory to inspire you to move ahead.

Reflect on a time when you were scared but did something despite the fear. How did you gather the strength? You can also think of someone you admire who displayed courage and jot down your thoughts about how they overcome their fears and what kinds of rewards they get from acting bravely.

______________________________________________

______________________________________________

______________________________________________

______________________________________________

______________________________________________

**Acting Opposite**

DBT is all about dialectical thinking – bringing together opposites. Here we can validate how hard it is and be kind to ourselves and compassionate towards the parts of us that want to give up. At the same time, we can recognize that avoiding is not the most effective path to take in life if we want to meet our goals. While we might understand this impulse, we do not need to act upon it.

If you need to pump yourself up, talk to some encouraging friends and have them remind you of your strengths, listen to some music that gets you in a more confident mood, and know that through this workbook, you will continue to work on skills to tolerate the discomfort of vulnerability. It's really the best option if you want to have a fulfilling life.

Recognize your urge to avoid, offer yourself validation and then mindfully practice doing the opposite. *Opposite Action* is a skill we use when we know that our behaviors and urges are not effective for meeting our goals or are based on faulty thinking.

An example. Many people talk themselves out of trying to date because they think they'll never meet the "right" person. This reflects a feeling of hopelessness that is understandable, but not based on logical thinking. The reality is. there are so many people looking for a loving relationship with whom you can create a positive connection. "The one," is just a myth.

I recently heard dating coach, Matthew Hussey, drop this wisdom in an interview: "You don't find the one, you make someone into the one."[16] It is up to each of us to find a compatible partner and make the effort to turn them into the one we want to be with by putting in the work.

So, in this case, *acting opposite* of the hopelessness would mean we acknowledge the fear but check the facts and act on what is achievable. Not looking for "the one" but bringing a willingness to find someone who wants similar things in life, shares similar values, and with whom you have fun and feel free to be yourself.

There is no fairytale and there will be conflict, there will be misunderstanding. If both of you approach these challenges in good faith, with fairness, and healthy communication, there will be growth and joy as well. Don't let fears of an imperfect relationship talk you out of looking for and creating a good relationship.

Similarly, don't let your own perfectionism talk you into waiting until you achieve all your self-improvement goals before going out to meet people. In her book, *How to Not Die Alone*, Logan Ury discusses the three different types of people who tend to struggle to build long-term relationships: *romanticizers* who hold overly idealistic and unrealistic expectations of relationships; *maximizers* who have unrealistic expectations of their mates and want to be certain they are with the right person before committing to someone; and *hesitators* who have perfectionistic expectations of themselves and put off dating until they are in their ideal mental, physical state or stage of life, which too often means, they never date.[17]

**Check the Facts**

If you are a hesitator who is getting in your own way and waiting for things to feel "just right" before starting to date, use the following skills to act opposite of this pattern. I also highly recommend Ury's book, which is chock-full of science-based suggestions for creating lasting, loving relationships for all three types.

The following exercise is designed to help you challenge false stories and take positive action despite feelings of reluctance or fear.

What are you avoiding? Write down what it is specifically you're avoiding acting on—is it joining an app or setting up your dating profile? Is it messaging with people? Is it moving off communicating on the app into real life meetups?

________________________________________

________________________________________

*example 1: I feel nervous about creating a dating profile*

*example 2: I am avoiding meeting up with anyone in person*

What is the story you are telling yourself about this action that is contributing to avoidance?

________________________________________

________________________________________

*example 1: I am trying to lose weight and want to wait until I feel better about my body.*

*example 2: What's the point? It never works out; all the available guys are avoidant and won't want to commit.*

Re-write this story to only include facts and to be accurate based on information available to you—no predicting the future, mind-reading, over-generalizing, catastrophizing. Just the facts.

______________________________________________

______________________________________________

*example 1: I am not feeling great about myself &I worry others will feel the same. I can pursue health goals while dating. People are attracted to all kinds of body types.*

*example 2: The last few people I have dated haven't followed through on plans or have been poor communicators. I feel frustrated. But I can choose to only date people who are consistent and communicative.*

What are your interpretations (thoughts, beliefs, assumptions) about these facts that turn this into the discouraging story you are telling yourself? What cultural, family, social, or relational experiences from your past influence these interpretations?

______________________________________________

______________________________________________

*example 1: I feel worried about experiencing rejection again so avoiding and giving up feels safer than trying.*

*example 2: I have been very hurt in past relationships and have fears that a long-term relationship is just not in the cards for me. I feel discouraged and scared that I will be left without warning, again.*

What are some small steps you can take towards healing this experience and belief?

*example 1: I can remind myself that I can choose who to trust and open up to. I can choose to be around kind and accepting people and set boundaries with anyone who is judgmental.*

*example 2: While there is no guarantee that I won't be hurt again by someone else, I can be more aware and proactive about setting healthy boundaries and upholding my standards rather than tolerating unkind behaviors.*

Would you be willing to be open to what might be possible outside of your past experiences and cultural, social, and family messages about love and relationships? If so, what are some other possible outcomes for you?

_______________________________________________

_______________________________________________

*example 1: I suppose I might meet someone who is kind and understanding, and who supports my goals while accepting me as I am now.*

*example 2: If I stay true to my values and uphold my standards then I could maybe meet a quality partner or at least build up my confidence and inner strength around setting healthy boundaries when I practice saying "no" to red flags.*

What is the worst-case scenario that could realistically happen?

_______________________________________________

_______________________________________________

_______________________________________________

*example 1: My fear is that I will meet someone I really like, they act interested, but then when I pursue them further they say something insulting or reject me.*

*example 2: I am worried I will get emotionally invested and close to someone who doesn't have my back like I did in my last relationship.*

How would you effectively cope with this experience if it were to happen?

____________________________________________

____________________________________________

____________________________________________

*example 1: I would call some of my most supportive friends to vent. I would talk to my therapist. I would cry and watch movies.*

*example 2: I will focus on what I gave and how I showed up as proof of my ability to be in healthy relationship and will date again when ready.*

What emotions come up for you now when you think about taking the step you are avoiding?

____________________________________________

____________________________________________

*example 1: I feel a little more confident even if still nervous.*

*example 2: Scared, reluctant, frustrated.*

You may have found that after working through your feelings and thoughts, your resistance has lessened and there is more willingness to take the next steps in your dating journey. But even if the avoidance is still there, we can use the next skill to move forward in a dialectical way—accepting and validating our emotions but acting opposite, one step at a time.

**VITALS: How to do something you don't want to do**

*VITALS* is a skill developed by Meggan Moorhead, Norma Safransky, and Bill Wilkerson, and adapted here for this workbook—it's meant to help us break through resistance and stop avoiding what Wise Mind knows we need to do.[18]

[19]

"Courage is: feeling afraid, diving in anyway, and transforming."

KATE SWOBODA

If your life goals and priorities include having a loving relationship, VITALS can help you break this down into smaller and more approachable steps and encourage yourself to make progress at your own pace.

Validate –write a sentence or two about how you are feeling and offer some validating and compassionate words towards yourself about that feeling. Acknowledge and accept that you feel resistance, rather than trying to push it away. What might you say to a friend feeling this way?

___

___

Imagine—mentally rehearse facing and completing what you are avoiding. Visualize yourself doing it confidently and successfully. Picture in as much detail what it takes to get through this process, step by step. Are you able to imagine yourself taking the steps you need to take? Record any reactions or reflection that come up from this step:

___

___

___

Take the first small step, then the next—what is the smallest first step you can take to just start some movement towards your goal? Break it up into mini goals, for instance, if it's creating a profile, step one could be asking a friend to help take photos or to assist you in writing or edit the content. Identify some of the steps on the lines below:

______________________________________________

______________________________________________

Applaud and Affirm yourself—watch your self-talk and make sure it is encouraging. Again, how might you cheer on a friend as they make progress? As you take the above steps, make sure you are speaking kindly and positively to yourself. Write down some supportive statements below:

______________________________________________

______________________________________________

Lighten the load—remind yourself of why you are doing this despite the fears. What will be the benefits? Will you make yourself feel proud? Will it improve an area of your life? Will it bring relief of no longer having to avoid? Will it bring the potential for new love and relationships in your life?

______________________________________________

______________________________________________

______________________________________________

Sweeten the deal—Build in rewards when possible—during or after your task. Savor the feeling of accomplishment by praising yourself or set up mini rewards when small steps are completed, such as a TV break, a piece of chocolate, or a nap:

_______________________________________________

_______________________________________________

Are you ready to move dating from online apps to real life? Even if you think you aren't ready, it might be time to venture out and take some risks. Nervousness is normal and with a little bit of mindfulness, interpersonal effectiveness, distress tolerance, and emotion regulation skills you can do this. DBT skills have got you covered!

CHAPTER THREE

# *On the Date and On the Apps*

## Describe and Accept Emotions to Expand Resilience

One important building block to cultivating *Emotion Regulation* is learning to accurately name and non-judgmentally acknowledge our emotions. Research shows that this on its own can already reduce the intensity and overwhelm of emotions.

We looked at some emotion words in the Chapter One, when imagining the kind of experience of relationship that we aspire towards. Let's do the same as we approach the dating experience. What emotions come up for you when thinking about meeting new people and using online dating apps? Can you put a few words onto your feelings.

---

---

*for example: I worry that dating will burn me out and that I will get really frustrated. I am tired of going on lots of first dates.*

Now write out a statement that is self-validating. Look for and re-write any judgments about yourself or your emotions.

___

___

*for example: It's ok to feel frustrated. I may need to vent to friends or take breaks from dating sometimes. Maybe I'll meet some interesting people or have cool experiences.*

How will this help you while dating? Tuning into and tracking your emotions can:

1) make you aware of your needs.

2) give you information about the quality of connections you are making.

3) alert you to the need to practice self-soothing or coping skills.

4) help you stay aware of the kinds of situations that lead to distressing or heightened emotions so you can make healthy choices.

**Pacing intimacy to promote Wise Mind**

A word about item 4 above. Emotion dysregulation can look like avoidance behaviors, anger outbursts, acting on impulsive urges, harshness towards self or others, shame or self-hate spirals, and self-harming behaviors.

Importantly, dysregulation can *also* look like elation and excitement that that brings on a feeling of intense craving and urgency. Even though this can feel pleasurable, in emotion mind it is easy to rush into an attachment and to set up a dynamic where we are looking for our next "hit" of positive attention or affirmation from our mate to quell our fears and inflate our hope.

Underneath the thrill of diving headfirst into a new relationship we often find a chaotic of swirl of emotion, including excitement, hope, and fear. When we move quickly into a new romance, it's harder to see all the facts and to make an informed decision.

We can reduce our vulnerability factors by making decisions that support a more balanced biochemistry. Hurrying intimacy increases the flood of neurotransmitters that take us out of calm and cool into the haze of the honeymoon phase. With Emotion Regulation skills like mindfulness of emotions we can notice our urge to speed ahead into a brand-new connection and, instead, make a Wise Mind choice. This might look like pumping the brakes so that we can more slowly savor the positive feelings and take a more measured approach to build a solid foundation that considers both facts and feelings. When we slow down it's easier to assess true compatibility.

While rushing a connection can heighten emotions and contribute to impulsive decisions, prolonging the online courtship process can also lead to heightened expectations and emotions. If we get invested in someone without having enough information to know their true characteristics and compatibility, we can easily start to fantasize about a person we have invented. At best, we'll likely feel disappointment when we meet them in person, and they don't match our expectations. Worse, having this image we've created and fallen in love with can cause us to ignore their real-life qualities that are harmful or aren't a good fit, so that we may preserve our fantasy version. For this reason, finding a balance in both building enough of a connection, but not delaying and giving so much time to fantasize, can promote Emotion Regulation. For many, it will be most emotionally healthy to meet in person after you've had enough conversation of substance to know there is a genuine connection, without letting too much time elapse before scheduling a first date.

**Spark versus substance**

Importantly, when I encourage meeting in person, it is not to see if there is a "spark." While it doesn't bode well if you are absolutely unattracted to your date, eliminating someone early on because there isn't "chemistry" is not a great way to date. Chemistry often takes time to build as emotional and intellectual closeness builds. Logan Ury confirms that the slow burn can be the more promising way to build a lasting relationship and cites research that of four hundred people surveyed, only 11% felt a spark or "love at first sight" upon meeting.[20] Attraction comes with feeling comfortable and close to someone, which takes time and patience. What in-person quality time allows us to do is build intimacy and closeness, to experience the fullness of each other, and to flirt and start to build a physical connection that is so essential for most of us in long-term loving relationships.

For those prone to emotional highs and lows, consider other aspects of pacing before starting to date. When you feel an immediate lightning bolt of attraction to someone, it can be tempting to spend several hours with them on the first date, then see them for consecutive days after. The excitement can be intoxicating. However, excitement is not an accurate measure of compatibility, and the intoxication has a similar affect as when we are drunk on alcohol—discernment is clouded.

To set yourself up for steadiness and sound decisions, keep the first date a couple hours in duration and space the first few dates out a few days to a week. This helps us slow down to assess what is real and consistent over time versus what is based on limerence, the neurochemical cocktail of lust and attraction.

When you meet someone and start to get closer to them, check in with Wise Mind to make sure you are staying committed to your own needs and giving yourself the space to get to know the person, rather than falling fast for a fantasy. When we don't know information about someone, we tend to fill in the blanks with our own narrative, and this can be skewed by our emotional investment, excitement, and hope.

I like to think of the first date as an initial low-pressure meeting to see if we would like to go on a romantic date. While a coffee date in a well-lit café often feels like a sterile setting that gives off interview vibes, sharing a stroll in a beautiful park or a cocktail in an atmospheric bar can foster intimate conversation. These situations also allow you to cut the date short if you feel uncomfortable in a way that a dinner date won't. You can also opt for an activity like mini golf, frisbee, going to a museum, or arcade, which give a sense of novelty and can be a more relaxing setting.

In sum, have a standard for who you meet, but then meet sooner than later, and move slowly, stay grounded and take your time to really getting to know your date. There is no rush—if someone is going to be your person, they will savor the experience of getting to know you and will build trust and safety over time. And you will be consciously choosing someone from Wise Mind, rather having someone chosen for you by an addictive urge to feel excitement or positive attention.

**Fun early date ideas:**

Atmospheric restaurant or bar for dinner/dessert/drinks
Mini golf
Bowling
Board game bar or (b)arcade
Wine tasting
Museum or gallery
Escape room
VR activity
Karaoke
Play Esther Perel's game, *Where Should We Begin*, or the *Ungame*
A walk or picnic at a botanical garden or public park
Art or cooking class

Comedy show
Live music

Again, Emotion Regulation does not mean that we get rid of our feelings, but rather, that we positively influence emotions through healthy choices, that we are able to recognize them for what they are—temporary biochemical processes—and gather any helpful information from them without being controlled by them. We can integrate them with the facts to proceed with Wise Mind.

After pausing to identify and validate your emotions and thinking of ways to stay anchored to Wise Mind, reflect on your readiness to take the next steps. Are you set to sign up for some dating apps, attend a speed dating event, and schedule some first dates? Maybe you've already done this and are jumping back in after a break. Or you've been on the dating scene all along and now are just more prepared with some skills.

Equipped with the self-knowledge of your needs in relationship and your values and priorities in life, it's time to make connections and schedule dates. Wise Mind can be your compass in your quest for love. Aim to find someone whose positive characteristics, communication efforts, and actions between dates matches the positive emotions you feel about them.

**Matching Mindfully: What and How skills**

While meeting potential mates online or in real life, practice dialectical thinking—holding the opposites of keeping your long-term goals in mind while also being able to drop an agenda so you can enjoy the present moment and stay open and curious about who you are getting to know. If you overfocus on your criteria for a long-term relationship early in the dating process, you may hastily rule someone out before getting to know them, jump to conclusions based on personal biases, or wind-up treating dates like interviews. Mindfulness can help us to stay in the present as we peruse dating platforms and chat up strangers.

DBT creator, Marsha Linehan, breaks down mindfulness into the smaller steps of what we do when we are mindful (the "what" skills), and how we do those things (the "how" skills). The "what" skills are *Observe, Describe*, and *Participate*. Observing means we take a step back from our immediate experience and just notice it without words. Describing means we add language to explain our experience of what we observe. Participating means we are fully engaged in our present experience.

The "how" skills are *Non-Judgmentally, One-Mindfully*, and *Effectively* and these are how we practice the above "what" skills. Non-judgmental means we stop labeling our experience, ourselves, others, etc. as "good" or "bad" and instead note just the facts. One-mindfully helps us stay in the moment and direct our attention to what is happening or what we are doing in the now. Focus awareness on whatever you are doing in that moment. When eating taste each bite and notice the sensations and textures of the experience. When taking a shower, feel the water on your skin and smell the soap, rather than planning your day or thinking about the past. Effectively asks us to think about our goals and do what will work best to meet them and to let go of being "right" if it undermines our long-term goals.

While this workbook isn't designed to be an authority on swiping strategies or polishing your online dating profile, here's how we might apply "what" and "how" skills so that we have some general guidelines to help us be more effective.

When we observe and describe non-judgmentally, we can bring an attitude of curiosity to dating apps rather than making snap judgments. With mindfulness skills you can counter the impulse to dismiss people quickly based on the very superficial information that the dating apps emphasize. At the other end of the spectrum, using a mindful approach, you can observe when you are overemphasizing surface qualities such as attractiveness and charisma. Dating apps are set up to highlight the features that matter the least in finding a compatible mate and are designed to mimic a consumer experience –allowing us to choose a person as if they are a product, based on limited details that don't tend to predict relationship satisfaction.

When someone's profile draws you in, remind yourself that you don't have the information you need to know whether they are a quality match for you. Observe and describe the feeling of desire, without letting that emotion decide what that means about compatibility. Remember, we cannot describe someone else's thoughts, feelings, character, or intentions just by observing them through their 2-dimensional profile. We can only learn this information from what they share with us and show us over time. Staying with the observe and describe skills, we can see what we know to be true versus what we are hoping will be true about someone with whom we match. We don't need to be suspicious of a match's motives or assume the worst but being mindful would mean bringing a blank slate to your interactions, rather than projecting an idealized image.

Some ideas that Logan Ury suggests in her book, *How to Not Die Alone*, can encourage us to practice the non-judgmental skill: expand your search filters to be more generous on height limits and age ranges, and don't discount someone based on a first impression in a photo, their occupation, or differing hobbies.[21] I worked with a client who thought she needed a partner who would accompany her to all her yoga classes and meditation retreats but making this a requirement drastically limited her choices. When a dating service set her up with a kind and thoughtful woman who had vastly different interests, she was pleasantly surprised by how much their values and goals in life meshed. They have been able to build a fulfilling relationship that includes togetherness through cooking, watching films, gardening, while they each continue to have robust lives independently that allow them to pursue their own unique interests. Be aware of your preferences and recognize when some of these preferences are non-essential and may get in the way of finding someone who could be a wonderful partner.

Think back to the values you identified, and the emotions you want to feel with your special someone. These can only be determined over time, through meaningful interactions, not through lists of their favorite movies or bands.

Are there any superficial qualities that have caused you to reject or eliminate a potential match? Practice being non-judgmental towards these. Reflect here and change your filter settings accordingly and start giving these folks a chance!

---

---

What are the positive qualities that hook you in and could lead you to overlook red flags or incompatibilities?

---

---

How can we bring the mindfulness skill of participate into our dating efforts? The participate skill asks us to forget our criteria and judgments, invites us to drop worries about the past and future, and place our attention to what is happening in the moment and engage fully in whatever it is we are doing. This could look like showing up interested and attentive in your back-and-forth pre-date communication, or it could also mean getting out into the real world and meeting people the old-fashioned way!

With the pandemic and overreliance of social media as a source of connection, many people have forgotten how to initiate conversation with strangers and may be out of practice having robust conversation with new companions. Even as far back as the year 2000, sociologist Robert Putnam's book, *Bowling Alone*, offered commentary on the decline of community in the US. Putnam's book discussed the increasing isolation of individuals, the disintegration of social bonds during a time when membership in bowling leagues, civic clubs, neighborhood organizations, etc. have sharply fallen off.[22] This trend has only increased in recent years.

Meeting people organically lends itself to more patience and open-mindedness. When we encounter someone at an event, we already know there is a shared interest, and we can't just swipe left based on a 3 second glance at their face. We interact with them as a whole person, and therefore can give them a chance to be a whole person, rather than a 2-dimensional profile with a few witty bullet points. Get a taste for what this kind of interaction can be like and bring this approach to online dating.

Participating fully in our lives will also mean we can bring a lot of value to our next relationship—by having unique experiences, perspectives, and a passion for life that will enhance someone else's life. It will also provide the opportunity to practice conversational skills and build new connections. Bonus if you make organic connections in real life that lead to a date—this can often be much more promising than a connection we make based on surface level info on an app.

Some ideas to try out the participate skill:

- Stop scrolling!!!! Seriously, take breaks from your phone/screen time—this can be hours, a day, or an occasional week away. It will be good for your brain!

- Practice being with yourself in the present moment and noticing emotions and sensations in your body without judgment or aversion.
- When out with friends or socializing in public, practice noticing emotions and thoughts of loneliness/longing/anxiety or behaviors like scanning the room for an attractive mate, and then sending yourself compassion for these emotions and experiences. These feelings are coming from a part that wants connection but have the result of taking you out of the moment, where you can most connect with yourself and your present experience. Acknowledge when these feelings arise, then come back to be fully engaged with the activity you're doing and people you're with.
- Listen to podcasts, read books, watch movies, and engage in activities that help you have some interesting topics to talk about when you meet new folks. Discover your genuine likes, interests, and follow those curiosities.
- Join Meetup.com and go to a few events that get you interacting with new people, start a conversation with a couple people at each event. Notice worries as they come up, validate the feelings, observe that thoughts are likely based in emotion mind, and gently return to the present.
- Find a social cause or volunteer opportunity you care about and go to their meetings and events, strike up conversation with a couple of people and be curious to discover your shared values.
- Go to a museum or cultural event on your own and approach someone who looks friendly and have a short chat with them.
- Take a local class—there are so many to choose from! Pottery, painting, dance, cooking, comedy, etc. I met one of my best partners ever at an acting improv class! I was terrible at improv but had a lot of fun—allow yourself to be not good at something and do it for the enjoyment and experience.

- Set up time to meet one on one with a couple friends and practice engaged conversation and active listening with them—need ideas for topics to discuss? Ask them a few of what the New York Times identifies as "the 36 questions that lead to love" to get to know them better or try the Ungame or Esther Perel's card game, Where Should We Begin?[23]

Jot down some ideas of activities or experiences you'd like to participate in, both to practice social connection and to develop a full life that you would feel excited to share with someone. What meetup groups, community events, volunteer opportunities, etc. would you like to try out?

______________________________________________

______________________________________________

______________________________________________

Great! Now go ahead and put some of these on your schedule!

**Participate while on your date**

Now that you've practiced participating mindfully in your own life and on the dating platforms, bring this skill with you when you meet your matches IRL (in real life).. While going out with someone new, do your best to participate one-mindfully, non-judgmentally, and effectively. Throw yourself into your experience as fully as you can while suspending judgments. This doesn't mean that you shouldn't be discerning about whether you feel safe or not with the person or in the environment. Please do not hesitate to leave a situation if it's sketchy. Judgmentalness is different from discernment, though. If you are getting caught up in thoughts that parse and evaluate everything the person is saying, how they are dressed, their mannerisms, or evaluating an imaginary future together, that will get in the way of participating in the moment. Discern whether you feel safe and okay spending time with the person but do your best to practice non-judgmentalness. If your mind is active and it is too hard to quiet thoughts to get to participation, try practicing the other mindfulness *what* skills: Observe and Describe.

**Meeting Mindfully**

The DBT mindfulness skills of observe and describe can both reduce anxiety when meeting someone new and at the same time can help you to show up in a way that other people will find refreshing and likeable. While we should not change who we are or be inauthentic to be likeable, it *is* healthy to be skillful and effective at building relationships, which does require an understanding and practice of qualities and traits that make people feel safe, included, and cared for.

Observing mindfully means that we watch the experience as it is unfolding in real time, rather than thinking about future fears, potential red flags, what-ifs, or our own self-criticisms and insecurities. With observe and describe, you can notice your self-conscious and worry thoughts if they arise, and then come back to observing what you are seeing, hearing, and sensing around you in each moment. You can notice your companion's facial expressions, nonverbal cues, or environment around you. Take in the whole experience through your senses without having to evaluate and make any decisions.

It is very normal to feel a little anxiety when meeting someone new. Soothe your nerves by validating your experience and continually coming back to what is happening in the moment. When you catch your mind drifting to self-doubt or scrutiny of your companion, observe your thoughts without trying to hold onto or get rid of them, and then gently turn your attention back to a nonjudgmental fact-based view of what is occurring in the here and now. When you bring your full focus to seeing and being with someone, there is less space for worries and self-conscious thoughts.

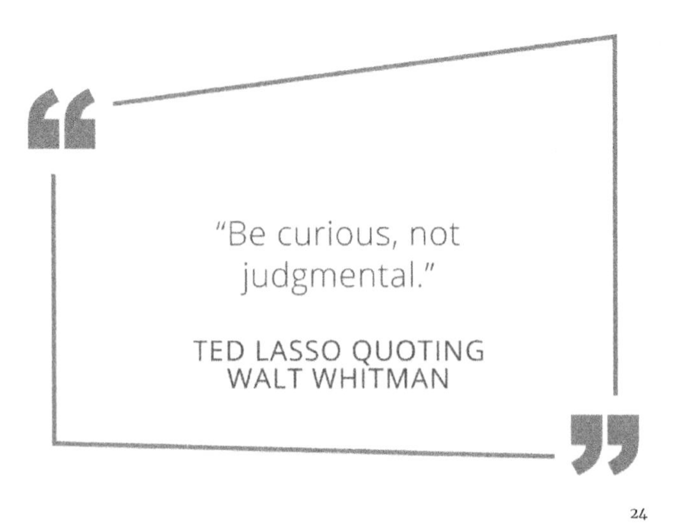


24

At the same time, the recipient of your attention will feel the difference between your presence and the usual half listening most of us tend to experience in day-to-day interactions. When you listen to others as if what they have to say is important, they will feel heard, engaged, and connected.

**Get out of your mind and into your body**

If your worry or judging thoughts are loud, and it feels hard to focus on the external you can also turn the observe skill inward but away from the mind and towards body sensations. Scan the body to notice where you feel either tension, ease, or something neutral. Try taking some full belly breaths and exhale long slow breaths to reduce the heart rate as you imagine creating space in your body for whatever sensations are arising. Practice allowing the present moment experience to be just as it is, without judgment or trying to change it.

You can try moving your awareness between your internal and external experience so that you can at once be attentive to your own inner experience while also continuing to engage with your date. As you observe what's happening internally, acknowledge without judgment. As you shift to paying attention to what's outside of you, try seeing, hearing, experiencing through your senses without making judgments and interpretations. Stay curious.

You can use the observe skill to notice what you find attractive in someone. Observe whether you are interpreting that attraction as a sign that you're meant to be together. Move your attention back to your body to observe your heart rate, breath, and sensations.

You can ask yourself: do I feel calm and relaxed? Is there a place in my body where there is ease? If there is tension, notice it and breathe into it without judging it.

Mindfulness skills will be easier to put into use on a date if you start practicing now. Take a moment to pause and look around, listen to the sounds around you, take in what is happening through your senses. Attempt to just witness and describe with factual language. What do you notice? Re-describe without any judgments if needed. Just the facts.

______________________________________________

______________________________________________

______________________________________________

Turn inward now and scan your body head to toe for any sensations and emotions, Observe and describe the experience factually.

______________________________________________

______________________________________________

______________________________________________

Work to practice being neutral towards your own emotions, sensations, and thoughts. It's okay that they are there exactly as they are. We can hold space for what is coming up without giving these feelings the power to dictate our actions. Remember, don't judge your judging!

**Cope Ahead for dating nerves and jitters**

Research has shown that mental rehearsal is an effective technique that can improve performance and reduce distress in high demand situations. Used in athletics and corporate settings, mental rehearsal involves what it sounds like—practicing successfully getting through a challenging experience with the power of imagination. If dating is something that causes nervousness, use this skill to "cope ahead."

Visualize yourself in as much vivid detail as you can—what you look like, what your body language is, what you are doing to get through the experience of meeting someone new. Notice yourself engaged and listening, picture yourself enjoying time with your companion and feeling confident and at ease. You can play this out like a movie you're watching in your mind and do your best to feel in your body the comfort and courage it takes to put yourself out there.

When you have a date scheduled, consider what you'll wear to feel your best, how you will behave, things you may ask or say that show you're engaged and curious. Notice how you will feel in your body when you know you are worthy of love and have many strengths. You can think of a few different scenarios and visualize moving through those effectively. Imagine how you might cope if your date is late, is rude, or if you get very nervous. Slow down and connect to Wise Mind as you mentally practice navigating each situation in a way that feels authentic and realistic for you.

Take a few moments to reflect on what came up for you as you mentally rehearsed being successful on your date? What does successful mean when you consider your values and goals?

________________________________________________

________________________________________________

________________________________________________

*for example: My goal is to be authentic and kind, to ask questions and show interest and to focus on getting to know them rather than making them like me.*

Is there anything from this visualization exercise that will help ground you in your principles and confidence while on your date? A keyword/phrase/mantra that you can anchor yourself with when nerves come up?

---

---

*for example: I see myself standing tall and feeling relaxed and confident. I will say to myself "Breathe deep and be real."*

If something happens on the date that leads to embarrassment or awkwardness, or if you don't connect with your companion at all, how will you cope and get through the experience?

---

---

---

*for example: I will remind myself this is temporary and try to see the humor in the situation. I will say I have to get up early if I need to excuse myself and will text my friends after to get support.*

**More DBT skills for getting through anxiety on your date**

*Paced breathing:*

When we're anxious our breath tends to become faster and shallower. Paced breathing can shift us into a calmer state, engaging the parasympathetic nervous system (PNS) by emphasizing exhales. When we exhale, our heart rate decreases.

Here is the pattern of the breath: Start with an inhale for a count of 4-5 seconds and exhale for a count of 6-7 seconds. Find the combination that works for you, making sure to exhale longer and more slowly than you inhale.

*Half smile:*

Relax your facial muscles. Release tension in your jaw with a wide yawn and wiggle of the mouth. Send the signal to your brain that you feel at ease and calm with slightly upturn of your lips. Let your mouth settle into a soft and gentle half-smile.

*Act as if:*

How do you want to show up to your date? Confident, secure, excited, and exciting? This skill helps us mentally and physically shift into the space of already embodying these qualities.

If you were confident and knew yourself to be a great catch, how would you behave, what would your body language and posture be like? Would your breath be even, your chest open, your spine alert and relaxed? Make some physiological shifts—intentionally slow down your breathing, practice some gentle yoga backbends and move through your days leading up to your date with a tall spine and soft heart.

Is there a friend or a character from a tv, movie, or book who exudes the kind of self-assuredness you would like to have? If anyone comes to mind, channel their energy. Imagine you are already that confident, take it on and embody that.

You also may need to "act as if" you are enjoying dating and are feeling hopeful. Everyone has their moments of feeling fatigue over endless swiping and half-hearted conversations on dating apps or gets hit with burnout after several first date flops. Make an effort to set this aside or take a break from dating to recoup and shake off jadedness before getting out and meeting people in person.

Just as you want your date to show up engaged and interested in getting to know you, do your best to remove distractions and compartmentalize any cynicism about the dating process so you can be present, as well. It can be a huge turn off when someone complains about dating or bad-mouths their recent matches. Try to bring a spirit of openness and treat this as a fresh start with a new person. We all know dating is full of disappointments and strange or unpleasant interactions but swapping stories can take the focus away from getting to know each other and can bring a pessimistic tone to the date.

This is another opportunity to practice dialectical thinking: yes, dating suuuuuucks, in general, but we don't know if this specific date we are on will suck until we give it our best shot! So, hold the awareness of the fatigue while also bringing curiosity and attention to each individual meetup.

Finally, act as if you are secure, or working towards inner security, while not denying your true needs in relationship. This means you:

- Practice self-soothing and have coping tools to return to an emotional baseline of calm, curious, and open. What breathing exercises, sensory practices, somatic activities, meditations, pep talks with yourself, etc. that help you regulate your emotions? Make a list and remember to use these during the early stages of dating anxiety.
- Express your reasonable needs in a kind, compassionate, and clear way.
- Pace yourself and neither rush nor stall building emotional or sexual intimacy with someone. Be willing to open and share gradually and to rely and depend on someone who earns your trust.
- Bring a sense of "we"- thinking into relationships, seeing your date as someone you would like to be on your team, and finding solutions together that are mutually

beneficial, neither centering yourself nor abandoning the self.

- Be sensitive to both your own needs and the needs of others, show compassion towards yourself and your date.

**Safe and Successful Communication on the apps**

A poll conducted by Pew Research Center in 2020 found that 60 percent of women ages 18 to 34 reported experiencing harassing or boundary-crossing behaviors like unsolicited explicit photos and repeated attempts to contact them after expressing a lack of interest.[25] 71 percent of all survey respondents believe it's common for people on dating apps to lie about themselves and their traits to appear more attractive. These are just some, if not the most pleasant reasons to develop skills around clear communication, assertiveness, and boundary setting while dating. Interpersonal Effectiveness skills give guidance on how to express our needs, set expectations, and build healthy relationships.

For many who grew up in invalidating environments, it is common to dismiss our own intuition or gut feelings about a situation or to minimize our discomfort or need to feel safe. Or we may have been taught that expressing our needs in an assertive way is rude or selfish. Learn to internalize the knowledge that you have a right to say "no" to anyone and in any situation that doesn't feel comfortable or okay for you. You have a right to ask for something you need, as well.

If you are feeling unease with anyone's tone, language, or requests and demands on a dating app, respond with a firm and clear message letting them know you aren't interested. You can also just disengage and not respond at all if they are continuing to try to hook you in to get a reaction. Don't hesitate to block and report an account that is harassing you or sending inappropriate photos or messages. Thankfully, even though the people who do behave in this way really stand out because of their despicable behavior, overall, most people will behave in a decent manner on dating sites.

**Building mutual relationships**

Aside from harassment and other disrespectful behavior, pre-date communication on dating apps can be a frustrating and bewildering experience of milder annoyances. There are people who match who never reach out or respond to messages. Conversations that never get going, that fade out or that involve one-word answers. People who go on and on about themselves but never ask any questions to get to know you. It can seem like you're really vibing with someone when they up and disappear, or they seem to only want to be your texting buddy and never want to meet up for a date.

When sending initial messages on a dating app, you can mention a common interest and build conversation around that. Highlight something unique about the person that you're curious to learn more about and ask them questions. It's frustrating when we get minimal responses, like one-word answers or no questions about us in return. Don't waste too much time trying to engage someone who is offering so little. Focus on where there is give and take, mutual effort and interest, move on from the rest.

We can use some assertiveness skills to be upfront about what we are looking for in our profile and initial messages. You have the right to be clear about what you want, and there are ways to communicate needs without coming off as "needy." It is entirely reasonable to share explicitly whether you are looking for something long-term, monogamous, or casual and open and to be clear and upfront in your profile about whether you have long-term goals of marriage or kids. You can ask for a phone call or video chat before meeting up if that is your preference. Messaging something like: "Hey! I prefer to have a quick phone call before I meet up with anyone. Is there a time you'd be up for a chat this week?" clearly outlines your desire to talk on the phone as a rule you use to establish connection, rather than a demand you are solely putting onto that person. You can also ask, if you don't see any mention in their profile, "I am curious what your goals are here for dating? I am not looking to rush anything but hope to find a long-term partner." If someone receives statements like these as too "needy," there is probably an incompatibility in terms of effort and energy you each are willing to put into a building relationship, or a mismatch in what you are looking for in a partner. It is better to be real about what you are looking for and eliminate folks who aren't a good fit, rather than try to play it cool and act like you have fewer needs so you can be liked, only to find yourself in a relationship that really doesn't work for you.

Likewise, remember to take others at their word. If you are hoping to find someone to build a life with, and the profile you are looking at says they want something short term or a FWB situation and their photos convey a party lifestyle, you can swipe left. I have had clients continue to invest in a connection even after their date explicitly said things like, "I'm scared of commitment," or "I don't know if I'm ready for a relationship." Often someone will be honest and explicit about their limitations, but it can be easy to explain away or minimize when the attraction is strong or physical intimacy has set limerence into motion. When someone describes their own capacity for connecting and maintaining relationship, take in this information. Listen to what people say and believe them —you can save a lot of time and heartache this way.

As mentioned before, taking the conversation off the apps and into real life sooner than later can help reduce potential for getting emotionally invested in someone before you know what it's like to be around them. However, we also don't want to meet everyone we match with on the apps. We need to have some sort of way to filter out folks who are clearly not willing to invest time and effort. Do have some conversation before meeting, to make sure there is enough of a connection and curiosity in each other, and that you both are willing and ready to put in more energy into courtship than occasional banter over text. Once that basic contact, interest, and effort has been established, getting to know someone through spending face-to-face time with them is the most effective way to build a connection and assess compatibility.

Once you do schedule the first date, one way to approach it with less pressure is to think of it as a fun outing to determine whether you'd like to go on a romantic date. Before meeting in person, it's hard to know the potential for romantic feelings and attraction. You don't know if being around them feels relaxing and easy or tense and uncomfortable just by exchanging messages or even doing a video chat. Doing a novel and interesting activity together during the first meeting allows you to relax and take some of the pressure off treating the date like an interview.

**Interpersonal effectiveness—getting people to like you**

While "getting people to like you" might sound like manipulation, I think of it as understanding human psychology of interaction and relationship.

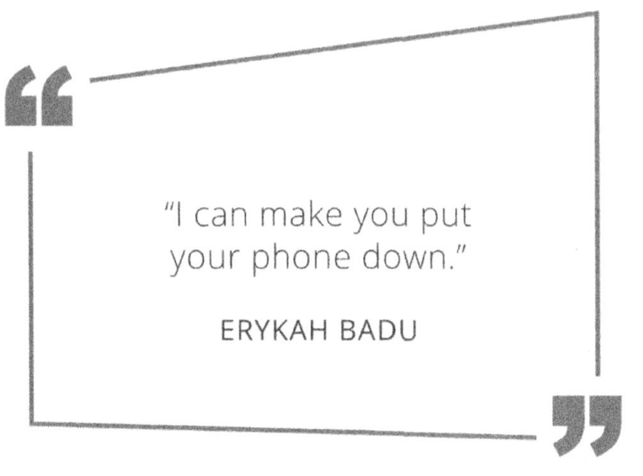


26

When we are interpersonally effective, we use our knowledge about people to be skillful and develop satisfying relationships. Most humans want to feel known and heard and understood. They want mutual and reciprocal caring connections.

So how can you show up to be that for others? Here are some suggestions.

- Be attentive and show interest in those around you.
- Don't multitask or check your phone when engaging with others.
- Focus on the present moment rather than preparing your reply.
- Ask questions, follow up on what people share, make it a conversation of give and take rather than an interview or interrogation.
- Respond to questions by sharing a little more information than is asked of you to keep the conversation going, maybe turn the topic back to the other person by asking about their experience with the same issue.
- Accept that small talk is a normal part of getting to know someone, and deeper conversation comes as we feel more trust and closeness with someone over time.
- Share private information that matches the level of openness of the other person—you can test out sharing a little more at a time and notice if your vulnerability is met with support and equal vulnerability to feel out the level of intimacy in your connection.
- Move your attention away from how you think you are being perceived, to taking in what others are saying and doing.
- Stay open and curious about what you don't know about someone.
- Observe any judgmental thoughts and let them go or replace them with factual description.
- Give people the benefit of the doubt and look for their positive traits.

- Participate fully in your conversations and activities.
- Act interested, ask questions, and validate.
- Be honest about your preferences and needs, and trust that they can handle the truth.

**Setting healthy boundaries**

Keep in mind that we can either have boundaries that are porous, rigid, or an appropriate balance of open with limits. When porous, we may tend to be quick to share the most private details of our trauma or past tragedies, and a date can then start to feel like a therapy session or will feel unidirectional to one of you. If we have porous boundaries, we may also be too willing to drop our own lives, commitments, or identities to merge with someone else—this can lead to a codependent dynamic where our sense of self is defined by the relationship rather than the relationship adding and enhancing to the wholeness we already are.

In a previous relationship, my porous boundaries, or what also could be called "self-abandonment," led me to make my partner's happiness my central focus, at the expense of myself. I created a dynamic in which I existed to support and encourage my partner. For years I focused on his life dreams, opportunities, and problems and did what I could to help him out. When I eventually started to share some of my goals and asked for support, my partner either grumbled at the hassle or accused me of being selfish and threatened to break up. While it is generous to want to help and support a partner, it isn't healthy to repeatedly give at one's own expense, while neglecting our own needs and goals as a separate individual.

In contrast, when our boundaries are too rigid, we may have walls up and avoid any vulnerable or emotional interactions and keep things light and surface level. We may start to withdraw or pull back after starting to feel close to someone, not ask someone for help or allow them to contribute to our lives when that would be meaningful for them. Letting someone in can sometimes feel like a threat to our autonomy or emotional safety, so going at a pace that continually moves towards more trust and intimacy and noticing but not acting on urges to run or shut down will be important.

To create balance, gauge the level of intimacy and share vulnerably up to a point that feels comfortable for the timeline of your relationship. Healthy boundaries allow closeness and intimacy to grow at a steadily increasing pace, without needing to either grasp on or push away. Keeping things overly light and keeping our distance can also get in the way of intimacy, so be willing to venture into some depth and vulnerability to foster authentic connection. Be real and open without oversharing or diving into all the heavy topics and issues right away, processing your past relationships, or sharing your deepest fears.

**The shit sandwich—a compassionate way to end a date when you're just not feeling it**

You've done the hard thing and you went on a date. Yay! Give yourself props for putting yourself out there. But what happens if you are out with someone, and you know that there isn't a love connection? What can you say to end the date or make it clear you aren't interested, while also being kind and respectful?

First, do your best to stay curious and open to at least enjoying yourself and getting to know your date as a fellow human, rather than convey any disappointment. Also, keep in mind it is common for people to show up awkward, nervous, and not completely themselves on the first date. If there was an obvious dealbreaker or you are feeling no potential to ever develop attraction to them, it's best to save their time and your own. However, recall the research from Logan Ury's book that found that 89% of people did not feel an initial "spark" with their now mate.[27] If the person you spent time with was kind, you enjoyed yourself, and you aren't turned off by them, it is probably worth giving it another shot to see if a romantic and sexual connection can grow.

It is true, though, sometimes *you just know* that someone is not for you. Sometimes it's clear that the lack of interest is mutual, and nothing needs to be said.

Other times, the person with whom you don't see a future still fancies you and asks you out on a 2nd or 3rd date. In these cases, I like to use what a friend of mine calls "the shit sandwich" to deliver the news in a gentle way. This sandwich is comprised of a layer of a thank you/positive feedback, a comment about your incompatibility, and some well wishes.

Do your best to be genuine and offer some tidbit that you truly did appreciate about them or the date. For example: "Thanks for going out with me, I had so much fun riding go-karts. I don't feel a romantic connection with you, but wish you the best of luck with everything," or "It was great getting to know you and learning about your amazing travels. I don't see us being a romantic match, but I hope you find the right person soon—I know you'll make an awesome partner." You can say it in person or wait until after to send a text. While they might be disappointed to learn that you are not interested, most people appreciate being told directly, rather than getting ghosted or strung along with indirect communication.

**Aggravating Apps & Disappointing Dates: Regulating Moods when Matching**

Whether we're dealing with fatigue from four hundred first dates, annoyance from confusing behaviors on dating apps, or anxious attachment urges after clicking with someone, emotion regulation skills can help anchor us back into feeling calm and present. An important way to modulate our emotions is simply to observe and describe them.

Take a moment to identify your emotions, rate the intensity, and notice the sensations that are present with it.

Emotion(s) I am feeling ________________________________

Intensity 0-100 (100 most intense, 0 neutral) ______

Sensations and location in the body:

_______________________________________________________

_______________________________________________________

Recall that a huge contributor to emotions are the stories we tell ourselves about events and situations. Be careful to not interpret someone else's unskillful actions, lack of interest, or poor communication as meaning anything about you or your worthiness. Take a moment to separate fact from fiction.

What is the event that prompted your emotions? Write an account as if you were a reporter only naming the who, what, when, where. Stick to the facts.

_______________________________________________________

_______________________________________________________

What are the stories and interpretations about these facts that you are telling yourself?

What are other possible explanations or outcomes that could happen?

If what you fear did happen, how would you overcome and cope? To whom would you turn to for support? What other external resources would get you through this? What internal resources can help you survive?

What would you say to a friend in this same situation, feeling what you are feeling? How would you validate them and show you care?

What are some simple pleasant and positive activities you can do right now? Practice being present and engaged in fun, interesting, exciting, or relaxing experiences, and letting go of worries.

________________________________________

________________________________________

________________________________________

When disappointment and burnout creep in, recommit to your values, and continue to make choices consistent with your long-term hopes and priorities. Remind yourself of your values and the goals you previously identified and make a note of ideas for how to shift your focus to self-efficacy (improving your confidence in setting and achieving goals and exercising your personal agency). Take small steps towards your dreams, and encourage yourself:

________________________________________

________________________________________

________________________________________

________________________________________

**Wise mind check-in**

While I have offered some suggestions in this chapter based on my own experiences, observations, and research, I do want to emphasize that you know yourself and what works for you better than anyone else. So many dating experts out there give conflicting advice, and there is no one right way to date. The timelines and ideas I recommend are meant to help reduce emotion dysregulation and to slow down your dating pace to allow you to connect with Wise Mind, rather than move full speed ahead into a relationship based on temporary and neurochemically influenced emotions. The most import DBT skill that you will have that should supersede any advice I give is your own Wise Mind awareness of what is the best choice for you. Connect with your values, your needs, and your Wise Mind to make decisions. When you drop into your own internal guidance, you may find that what feels right for you is different than what I recommend. What matters is that it feels safe, comfortable, and good for you.

Take a moment now to do a Wise Mind check in about where you are on your dating journey and your current needs. Start by noting how you feel. Then note the facts. Pause, breathe, and tune into your "hut" (heart + gut).[28]

What does Wise Mind say?

______________________________________________

______________________________________________

CHAPTER THREE

# After the Date

Congratulations! You've been on a date. Now what? In this chapter you'll find recommendations for surviving and skillfully navigating some of the most frequent dating scenarios. First, let's pause to reflect.

**Wise Mind Check-in**

After going out with someone is a great time to pause and check in with Wise Mind.

If we have just had a first or second date, we can keep things simple. It's too early to know someone in depth, but we may have an intuitive awareness of how we felt around them, and whether they made us comfortable and curious enough to want to see them again. I remember listening to a podcast years ago with dating coach, Evan Marc Katz. I love what he said. He suggested we ask the following after a date: 1. Did I have fun? 2. Could I be myself? 3. Do I feel attracted enough to see them again?[29] Katz also recommends rating your experience on a scale of 1-10 for each of these categories: Comfort, Fun, and Attractiveness, 10 being the best. While 10s across the board will be rare, determine a score that is both realistic and that would be a promising match for you. If comfort and fun are high on your scale, but attractiveness is lower, I would give the connection more time, because attraction often grows the more we feel emotionally connected with someone. After the first couple of encounters, having a basic formula like this can help us not spin out into rumination when it is too soon to have the information we need to assess compatibility.

Tune into your experience and ask Wise Mind:

- Was it positive, did I feel safe and enjoy myself?
- Could I be myself?
- Was I attracted enough to give it another go?

Write your reflections here, feel free to assign a number rating 1-10.

---

---

---

We might be surprised when we allow ourselves to set aside judgement and get to know the person we are dating from an open-minded and curious stance. Of course, if there are clear indicators that the person is not emotionally available or other red flags, then it will be crucial to let them know it isn't a good fit and move on as soon as possible.

**Real Red Flags**

If you observe any of the following in your date during your early interactions, consider ending things or proceed with extreme caution if you are trying to distinguish between a rare incident or a pattern:

- Impulsive and reckless behaviors
- Crosses a boundary, limit, or "no" that you set
- Anger outbursts/volatile temper towards you or others
- Superficially charming and overly romantic very early on
- Initiating intimacy without consent or without gauging your receptiveness
- Lack of interest and withholding of positive words, warmth, and affection
- Expects you to pay for all dates and doesn't reciprocate
- Pervasive identification as a victim and blaming outside factors or other people for all their problems
- Jealousy directed towards your interests, friendships, time spent on your work and attempts to change your involvement in those
- Unreliable and inconsistent
- Enmeshed in relationship with family or an ex
- Keeps you away from their friends, family, or important parts of their life
- Has an active addiction
- Abuse of any kind

Can you think of any others you would add?

______________________________________________

______________________________________________

Sometimes our behavior changes when we are with someone who feels unsafe or who is not a good match. This means the red flag might show up in how you are behaving and feeling after spending time with your date. This may not be apparent early on but there are things to watch out for in the weeks and months to come if a relationship develops. Step away from the relationship and consult with a professional if you notice you are:

- ➢ Avoiding raising your concerns or expressing your feelings for fear of conflict or displeasing them
- ➢ Feeling dependent or like a younger version of yourself around them
- ➢ Dissociating, disconnecting when with them
- ➢ Feeling like you are acting or performing around them
- ➢ Feeling very high highs and very low lows
- ➢ Giving way more than you receive from them
- ➢ Giving up friendships, interests, focusing most of your time, energy, attention on them at the expense of your own life and independence
- ➢ Neglecting your basic self-care and dropping the PLEASE skills
- ➢ Trying to generate feelings of closeness or connection through sexual intimacy that are otherwise missing
- ➢ Moving too quickly—whatever that means for you—cohabitating, marriage, or even discussing these as future goals. before the foundation is built and you know each other well
- ➢ Making excuses for their inappropriate behavior
- ➢ Coercing or trying to control or "fix" your partner

Any more you can think of? It might be useful to get feedback from a friend or therapist for ideas. Ask them what they have noticed as signs of concern when in your past unhealthy relationships.

____________________________________________

____________________________________________

After you've had a few dates, and comfort, fun, and attraction are still there, start to consider long-term compatibility factors. Check in with *Wise Mind* and reflect on the following:

Are your life goals and values aligned? Are your needs being met?

________________________________________

________________________________________

________________________________________

Are you behaving consistently with your own values while in this relationship?

________________________________________

________________________________________

Are you both able to navigate issues that come up effectively and fairly, without too much distress, angst, or hurt feelings?

________________________________________

________________________________________

________________________________________

On to the different scenarios you might find yourself in after a date or two. Don't see your specific circumstance here? Reading through some of the examples will help you adapt and apply the skills to other contexts. All of these sections are very interactive and invite you to reflect, engage in exercises, and write throughout. If you need a refresher on any skill that isn't explained, check out the appendix.

**Ahh! I think I embarrassed myself.**

Are you ruminating over things you said or replaying moments from your outing with a self-judging eye and critiquing how you looked, what you said or did? Going on a date can feel vulnerable. If we are nervous, we may trip up our words or not feel as confident as we would have liked. You are human, please be kind to yourself and use these skills:

Imagine what you would say to a friend in this situation and write it out here:

______________________________________________

______________________________________________

*Mindfulness of Emotions*—observe and describe *without any judgments* that you feel embarrassed, worried, upset, and validate the emotion. Notice the sensations in the body as they come and go. Allow your emotions to be present and tell yourself they will pass. Remind yourself of times you have made it through difficult feelings.

*Mindfulness of Thoughts*—observe and *describe without any judgments* the thoughts that are going through your mind. Notice that they are thoughts, driven by emotion mind. If it helps you to visualize them as clouds in a sky, or train cars on a track, or leaves in a stream, use your imagination to watch them pass by.

*Distract* with the ACCEPTS skills. Turn to engaging or fun activities or put your mind to work on something that will use your brain in a different way—like a crossword puzzle or math problem. Distract skills can also include using music, film, or art of any kind to evoke a different emotional state. You can also contribute to a friend or someone else in need, focusing your attention on their issue rather than your situation.

I will skillfully distract with

___________________________________________

___________________________________________

*Self-soothing* means using your senses to bring your nervous system down from a heightened state to one of more relaxation and ease. This could be a bubble bath, tea ritual, or a anything that works for you.

I will self-soothe by ____________________________

**Eep! I really like her/him/them**

Great! "Like" is an appropriate feeling to have about someone you're just getting to know and really hitting it off with! It makes sense to get excited and feel hopeful about this kind of connection. In DBT, we often stop back and reflect to ask, does our emotion fit the facts? And if you have met someone a couple times, are having great conversation, feel relaxed and at ease around them, and wouldn't mind making out, then the emotion of "really like" does fit the facts. Bravo! You've done the hard thing of putting yourself out there, and so far, so good.

Moving forward, rely on Wise Mind to make decisions that feel right for you, pace yourself to regulate your emotions, and manage expectations to allow for the relationship to unfold organically in natural time, and see where things go. Keep coming back to the values you want to build your life around and the emotions you want to feel in a relationship as a way to check the pulse and health of this connection as it grows.

Don't be afraid to tell someone you like spending time with them, are attracted to them, or to ask them out. Anyone who would be available for a secure relationship would welcome this direct communication and would be actively offering the same feedback to you.

What is your Wise Mind goal for building this connection over the next few weeks? What are the next steps that feel aligned with Wise Mind?

______________________________________________

______________________________________________

If you "really like" someone who gets your heart rate going, but find it hard to talk to them, or feel insecure around them, this might be a sign that the feelings do not fit the facts. It could be more accurate to say you wish you did really like them because you find them attractive. But really liking someone who has a negative impact on our self-esteem or with whom we can't hold a conversation is counterproductive and likely won't lead us to meet our relationship goals. As hard as it may be to pass on someone you find attractive, you're closer to finding a great match for you when you let go of someone who is a mismatch. Check in with *Wise Mind*.

**Ack! I think I'm in love with her/him/them!**

Okay, fellow hopeless romantics, this one is for you (and me). Bliss and elation can be just as dysregulating as anxiety and sadness. If you are very attracted to someone, feel strongly magnetized to them, and feel like you've known them forever, consider this a yellow flag, meaning it's wise to slow down.

For most people, neurochemicals create a blissful buzz or high in the early relationship stages. This stage of a relationship is called limerence and describes the infatuation we feel when the brain is flooded with dopamine, norepinephrine, and testosterone. Under this spell, we fixate on and crave being around our love interest and see them in the best possible light. While this certainly feels amazing, we must learn to make space for the joy of connection while also staying grounded enough to be discerning in our choices, and cautious in our commitments. It takes observing behaviors over time, in day-to-day life, and once the honeymoon stage has passed to truly evaluate the health of a relationship and understand the true character of a partner. Most of us project our best selves early in a relationship, and in the fog of infatuation, we are also less likely to pick up on red flags or notice when something is off from what we value or need.

For those of who have attachment injuries that can lead us attach quickly for a sense of security, reassurance, and to feel worthy/okay/loveable, this neurobiological experience can be dicey. It's okay to feel excited and anticipate spending time with your love interest, but they are just that—someone with whom you are interested in building love. Love takes time to grow into. So, if you are finding yourself feeling like you love someone you are only getting to know and are picturing a future together with them after only a few dates, it's time to pause and check if the emotion fits the facts.

Here are some examples of what Marsha Linehan, who developed DBT, says justifies feeling love for someone (paraphrasing her): When that person adds value to your life and improves your day-to-day experience of living. When loving them helps you move towards your own life goals. I would add that love fits the facts when we admire someone's values and the ways they have responded to life's challenges and opportunities. Also, when they treat people (including us) kindly and with respect.

When someone is brand new to you, it is hard to have enough knowledge of who they are, how they treat others, and what their values are. So, while the "in love" feeling is something we can experience early due to a lot of happy drugs in the brain, the emotion of love does not fit the facts—not the facts we have available right now, at least. For that, we just need more time, more patience, more curiosity to get to know them. Let's allow and nurture the connection through effort and willingness to understand the other and give them the opportunity to see and respect our vulnerability and values, as well.

When our feelings don't fit the facts, DBT encourages us is to act opposite. Acting opposite of love does not mean we act with hate. Rather, we focus on the urges that we have due to the emotion of love, and act opposite of those. Use the table on the next page for inspiration and fill out the blank rows to add your own.

| *Emotion Urge for Love* | *Opposite Action* |
|---|---|
| Fixate and obsess about love interest, replay romantic moments over and over, wonder if they feel the same. | Distract with positive activities, remind myself of how little I know them, call a friend to distract. |
| Keep checking phone for texts from them. | Turn phone off, take a break from electronics for a few hours, practice mindfulness exercises or paced breathing. |
| Think about marrying them, moving in with them, wondering when I can see them next. | Slow down the pace. Space out dates so that I'll be more connected to Wise Mind to see the situation more clearly. |
| Spend every minute with them, be in touch constantly when apart. | Take breaks from them. Devote time and energy to activities, things, and people who have enhanced my life before I met them. |
| Wonder what's wrong with me that I feel so intensely anxious and craving them. | Remind myself of the facts about limerence, validate my feelings. Work to build inner security within myself. |
| Think about how much I love them and need them. | Think about how much I need to take care of myself and make Wise Mind decisions. |
| | |
| | |
| | |

**Help! I'm getting mixed signals?!?!**

This kind of hot/cold and confusing behavior from someone never feels good! Instead of trying to psychoanalyze and figure them out, use this experience to:

*Distract or Self-soothe.* It is reasonable if a lack of consistency or availability activates an anxious response. When this causes dysregulation, look for ways to calm your nervous system and find ways to restore a sense of safety. Start with some comforting activities that engage the senses or activities that will redirect your attention to something positive. Look over these suggestions and then brainstorm some of your own that you know help bring your nervous system down from a heightened to more safe and relaxed state: walking in the woods and being mindful of the beauty around you, listening to a playlist of self-love and life-affirming jams, reading poetry, taking an Epsom salt bath with lit candles nearby, drinking a cup of tea from a favorite mug, calling a friend, cuddling my dogs or watching them play, getting under a weighted blanket... Can you come up with self-soothing ideas that work for you?

___

___

___

___

Access *Wise Mind* and reflect on what you want from a partner and return to the emotions you identified in the Chapter One indicating how you want to feel in relationship. If someone is being unclear, intermittently responsive, or contradicting their words with their actions, ask yourself—is this what I want from a partner/in a relationship? Are these the qualities that bode well for a long-term partner who is committed to being upfront and reliable? If not, worry less about the other person, and focus more on why you are putting up with this behavior. Reflect on what messages you've internalized that led you to think you must accept this treatment, or to assume that there's something you should or could be doing differently to capture their interest.

Obsessing about what someone else is thinking and feeling when they are not communicating clearly is exhausting and unhelpful. It's also a way of distracting yourself from taking responsibility for your own self-care. Hearing from them might bring relief, but it will be short-lived if mixed signals are part of their pattern, and you'll swing like a yo-yo in and out of calm and confusion unless you shift to meeting your own needs for connection. Train yourself to be turned off by unavailability, and to be attracted to consistent effort.

Confused? Ask. *Interpersonal effectiveness* skills give us a handy dandy cheat sheet on how to have difficult convos and ask hard questions. This skill is called (O) DEAR MAN:

- Opener (technically not part of the skill, but it's kinder to soften things with a greeting.) –Hey there! I hope you're having a great week.
- Describe the situation—I had a lot of fun on our dates. You said you were going to text to catch up and schedule another date for this weekend and I haven't heard from you yet.
- Express how you feel— I know you said things sometimes get busy with work, but I'd like to be in touch more consistently. Since it's been a couple days, I'm

wondering if you're still interested in going out or if you've decided to move on.

- **R**einforce (reward or specify consequences)—I am sure we will have a great time if you're up for it, but if you're not feeling a connection, or aren't able to be in contact between dates, I understand and wish you the best of luck!

Communicate this:

- **M**indfully
- **A**ppear confident even if you are nervous
- **N**egotiate if appropriate

Notice that in the "express" portion I did not divulge a lot of vulnerable and tender emotions. Nor did I take out my frustrations on them and express anger. Since this is early into a connection and I am already feeling insecure in this dynamic, I do not want to give that much power to someone who is either ambivalent or not invested in our connection. I also don't want to make that person responsible for my emotions, and instead, take appropriate action to problem solve by changing or leaving the dynamic that is causing these emotions.

Instead, I am only conveying what is important for them to know to understand my needs and requests. It is worth evaluating whether it is worth doing a DEAR MAN at all with someone you don't know well. If you've tried to reach out and they seem to be ghosting, ask *Wise Mind* whether it would be worth putting more energy into someone who isn't giving anything back. You might decide to reach out if there have been enough real positives and there are plausible reasons to make their behavior understandable. If it's the latter, give them the chance to apologize, explain, and improve their behavior, while stating your expectations around consistent communication.

Here is some space to write out a script, if you do choose to ODEAR MAN your date:

______________________________________________

______________________________________________

______________________________________________

______________________________________________

______________________________________________

*Observe your emotions and sensations and describe them non-judgmentally.* For instance, "I am noticing my throat is tight, my thoughts are racing, and I notice feelings of anxiety and worry."

You can add a self-validating statement, maybe something you would say to a friend in this situation: "It makes sense that I feel this way, and I am sorry it's so painful. I love and accept myself even thought I am feeling really upset." If this feels like a lie because you are judging yourself or your feelings, add that as an observation you describe: "I notice a part of me is judging the my anxiety. It makes sense because I was often judged as a kid for having strong feelings. I am learning that emotions communicate needs, and my needs are valid, even if they cannot be met in this moment." You can go back to the list of needs to name some that you have—say, reassurance, peace of mind, intimacy, understanding.

While we cannot demand or expect that someone we are dating will always be able to meet our needs, we can practice self-validating our own needs, and sharing them with compassionate others. Is there someone who cares and listens well who will say, "That makes so much sense. I want those for you, as well." You can start by being that person for yourself even as you long for more people in your life to show up with compassion and care. The more you are that friend or partner to trustworthy and caring people in your life, the more it will come back to you.

Practice observing and describing your own emotions non-judgmentally. Name and validate your needs:

___

___

___

*Opposite action!* Fear lets us know we could lose someone or something we care about. If it is a new connection, we may fear that the hope or fantasy we had built up is slipping away. If someone is not communicating with us, is not consistently showing interest, then the anxiety is picking up on something real, and fear fits the facts. However, check to see if the intensity of your anxiety fits the facts. Often the intense anxiety we feel in the present is rooted in something from our past. We can validate our feelings and direct compassion towards the parts of us that feel scared or sad, understanding that there is healing needed more from our past experiences than a need to fix this current one.

Similar as to described in the example on Love, above, if you are wanting to text and connect with someone who is showing little interest in connecting with you, your interest in them might not be appropriate or effective for the current reality. What are the actions opposite to ruminating about their inner emotions? This could be thinking about your own emotions, thinking about the emotions of your friends who do show up consistently for you, or this could be thinking about something else entirely that you find fascinating or fun. Opposite action would mean not reaching out to someone who is unresponsive, giving them the chance to put in the work to show they are interested. Jot down some of your urges when anxious and some possible opposite actions you can take when those emotions come up. I have offered some of examples as a starting point.

| *Emotion Urge for Anxiety* | *Opposite Action* |
|---|---|
| Wonder why they haven't texted back, think "they must not like me." | Write a list of possible other reasons why they might not have texted back, self-soothe, and distract. |
| Keep texting or calling until I hear back. | Call or text a friend instead, put my phone in another room, take a walk and leave my phone at home. |
| Keep checking their social media accounts to see if they've posted recently. | Mute their profile, temporarily delete social media apps from my phone. |
| Overanalyze every word in every text from them to figure out how they feel. | Check the facts—I can't know how someone feels from a text message, I can only describe what they said. |
| Ruminate about whether they like me, feel urgency around knowing or receiving a sign from them. | Radically accept that dating involves uncertainty, remind myself of times I have coped with uncertainty before. |
| | |
| | |
| | |

If someone is showing up and being communicative and we recognize that our anxiety is part of an old pattern, then we want to act opposite of anxious urges, as well. We can communicate our needs or share our experience, while maintaining healthy boundaries so that we do not shift the responsibility of regulating our emotions someone we are dating.

**Ouch! They aren't into me/ghosted me.**

When someone expresses a lack of interest or flat out disappears and stops communicating, this can be hurtful and confusing. *Check the facts* if you're having negative self-talk. Be mindful of thoughts—notice if you are getting caught in black and white thinking or catastrophizing from this experience. This could be any variation of one of the following: "All men/women/people are jerks," "Everyone good is taken in this city," "There must be something wrong with me," "I will always be alone," or "No one loves me."

When we have extreme thoughts with all or nothing sentiments, we know we are in emotion mind. It might feel impossible to shift into *Wise Mind* from here. Notice the emotion underneath the thoughts and practice *mindfulness of emotions*. Maybe you're feeling disappointment, frustration, sadness, confusion, anger, impatience, etc. It is reasonable to feel any or all these emotions. We don't want to use that emotion to come to drastic conclusions about ourselves, others, or life. Instead, practice some of the following:

*Ride the emotion wave*—observe your feelings and sensations as they arise and then pass. Bring curiosity to your experience. Mindfulness teacher, John Kabat-Zinn has said that: "You can't stop the waves, but you can learn how to surf."[30] Watch and notice how emotions show up in and move through your body, without trying to change or resist them. Know that the emotions will not last forever, and imagine yourself on a surfboard, riding out the wave of these feelings. Observe them non-judgmentally. Work to stay with your feelings, noticing how they show up and change, rather than going into the stories and interpretations in your head about the situation—stories like "This always happens, what's wrong with me?" (There is nothing wrong with you) or "What an asshole, he must be a narcissist" stick with the facts like "He never replied which is an unkind behavior and unacceptable to me. Therefore, I am moving on to find someone more communicative and interested in getting to know me." Direct compassion towards the parts of you that feel disappointed. Resist the urge to diagnose or label someone you don't know. It is natural to feel angry and can be a temporary boost to the ego to insult someone who has treated us poorly, but it will be more powerful to attend to your own pain and take care of yourself rather than continuing to focus on someone who is not concerned about you.

*Loving-kindness*—this originally is a Buddhist practice meant to encourage the cultivation of a compassionate state of mind towards all beings. In our minds, with the intention of generating warmth and kind wishes, we direct our loving thoughts towards ourselves and others. If we are in a low mood or feeling hard on ourselves, sometimes it is easiest to start with an animal or friend we love before turning the feeling of goodwill towards ourselves.

1. Sit, stand, or lay down and get comfortable.
2. Slow down and deepen your breath.
3. Bring a person or animal to mind who is easy for you to feel loving towards.
4. Notice the sensations that accompany positive emotions towards this person or animal, recite compassionate phrases that feel authentic for you, something along the lines of: "May you feel happy, healthy, and whole. May you be at peace and free from suffering." Repeat the phrases several times slowly, staying mindful of the

intent behind them and connecting to your positive feelings towards the person or creature.

5. Once you feel connected to the warm and compassionate feelings, turn these towards yourself, reciting a variation on the following words that resonate with you: "May I feel happy, healthy, and whole. May I be at peace and free from suffering." Repeat these words slowly and absorb their meaning in your body and mind.
6. If it feels right for you, the next step would be sharing the compassion generated from this practice with more beings, known and unknown. You can work through recitations of the words you came up with while you imagine directing loving energy towards people you know or strangers who may be going through similar experience and emotions as you, or anyone else at all who may need some loving-kindness.

*Distract or self-soothe*—Engage in fun, light, or engrossing activities that get your mind off the situation. Baking, roller skating, board games, crossword puzzles, knitting, dog walking, making art, putting a puzzle together, masturbating, dancing to your favorite songs, calling a friend, watching a movie, etc. You know best how you can distract yourself from negative self-talk or painful emotions. Self-soothing activities might be particularly helpful. Sipping hot cocoa, eating delish ice cream, taking a nap, taking a fragrant bath, or using aromatherapy, practicing visualization or guided meditation are just a few ideas to calm the nervous system.

*Radical Acceptance*— Most of my clients have a love/hate relationship with this skill. Radical Acceptance can be so freeing yet is so incredibly difficult. Remember, accepting is not the same as liking or approving of, but is facing the reality head-on and acknowledging the truth of it.

In times of heartbreak and relationship endings, it has helped me to tell myself, over and over until it sinks in: "The relationship is over, they don't want to be with me, they are gone and are not coming back." Sometimes this brings on sadness or pain, but when I allow this grief to be released, I can move forward instead of getting stuck in a fantasy." If it's very early in the connection, you may have to radically accept that a relationship you hoped was blossoming is now over, letting go of a dream: "I was hopeful about this connection. This connection is over. This is hard." Part of radical acceptance is allowing ourselves to feel the emotions that come up, accepting those as well. We do *not* radically accept our distorted thinking—such as "I will never find a partner." That is not a reality that can be proven but a catastrophic thought rooted in emotion mind. Try to identify the emotion behind the thought and work toward accepting that: "I feel very disappointed and hopeless. That's understandable but doesn't mean that there is no hope for the future." Accepting reality helps us to take effective action and get on with our lives. Some ideas for practicing radical acceptance include:

- notice that you are arguing with reality when you are in a story of "this shouldn't or can't be happening," or are thinking of strategies to re-connect with this person.
- repeatedly say aloud or write down the difficult truth you are working to accept.
- observe and allow the sensations and emotions that come up as you work towards acceptance.
- Imagine how would you act if you had accepted the reality and make choices and behave as if you already have accepted.
- engage your body in the process: open your arms wide lift your chest up, tit your head to the sky and notice the sensation of surrendering to what is.
- remind yourself that life can be meaningful and fulfilling even when we are experiencing rejection and hurt.

*Accumulate short and long-term positives*—Throw yourself into activities you enjoy and ground yourself in the relationships, values, and interests that make you who you are, independent of whether a romance pans out or not. Before you met this person you had a full and meaningful life. Do what you love and what brings you pleasure as if you had never met this person. Remind yourself of who you are and what your long-term goals and values are. Take steps towards those. If being in a loving relationship is one of those goals, tell yourself that stepping away and moving on from someone who doesn't want to be with you is moving you closer to the goal of finding the right relationship.

Use *Opposite Action* to climb out of the shame spiral—Rejection can sometimes lead to feelings of shame. Shame is an emotion that has, evolutionarily, helped us to survive by alerting us when we may have violated norms, rules, or ethics shared by a person or group. When we experience shame and it fits the facts, it is so that we can correct or repair if needed and not risk community exile or being cast out by someone we love. The problem is, too much of the time, we experience shame when it is unwarranted, or we hold onto it much longer than needed.

Often, the people whose expectations or ethics we've violated have not earned that important place in our life to judge us and our behaviors. In society, there are many norms that are based on regressive and oppressive notions of morality, sexuality, racism, classism, and personhood. If we truly have done something to upset the expectations of someone we love or respect, or we offended the culture of a group we value, then shame is a useful emotion to motivate us to take accountability and heal the relationship. But when someone you've dated decides to end things, this is not a reason to feel shame.

People often overdo shame and instead of using it for its intended action—to reflect and repair—instead berate and beat themselves up endlessly, which only causes more harm and helps nobody.

Let's check out some possible opposite actions to common urges of shame. Read through the examples and complete the table with your own ideas of urges and opposite actions you can do if this feeling arises in you.

| *Emotion Urge for Shame* | *Opposite Action* |
|---|---|
| Beat myself up with unkind thoughts, insult myself, believe the thought "there must be something wrong with me," or "I'm a failure." | Check the facts—think of times when friends, animals, family have expressed love for me. Call a friend and ask for support. |
| Tell myself to give up, delete the apps, and never date again. | Pause profiles for a short break, spend time with friends, doing positive activities, then get back to dating when ready. |
| Stay in bed and hide under the covers, stop leaving the house, neglect personal care. | Allow rest but also use VITALS or one-mindfully in the moment to keep up self-care. |
| Engage in distracting, self-avoiding or self-harming or impulsive behaviors. | TIPP skills. Radically accept this is a hard moment and practice Loving-Kindness towards myself. Seek support from a professional. |
| | |
| | |
| | |

*Use Opposite Action to be effective*—For some, shame is an immediate and powerful response to feeling rejection. Others might turn the judgment outward and express anger or hostility. There may be some situations where the anger does fit the facts—people behave poorly behind the anonymity of apps all the time, and you may have legitimate complaints. However, if someone ended things in an unkind way after a brief time together, it may be more effective to move forward rather than expending more energy making your case against them or expressing your anger to them directly.

If someone crossed a boundary or said something out of line, it can be appropriate to say something using DEAR MAN, (Describe, Express, Assert, Reinforce, Mindfully, Appear Confident, Negotiate) or perhaps more aptly, DEAR MA. Wait for the strongest of the emotions to pass, then state the facts, share briefly how you feel about it, and assert a boundary. No need to negotiate.

However, if it's early in the dating stages and someone suddenly expresses disinterest or disappears, resist the urge to act out on any anger through verbal attacks or aggressive outbursts. Self-validate and find healthy outlets for moving through the feelings. Think about your values and the kind of person you would like to be, and act as if, even if you aren't feeling that way.

**Shrug. I don't know if I like her/him/them.**

Hey, it's perfectly okay to be confused. After the first date we may be on the fence about whether to see someone again. Remember, it's natural for things to feel awkward and for us or the other person to be nervous upon meeting, so if no red flags are present, and none of your personal deal-breakers are there (say you met a smoker, but only date non-smokers or you learned they definitely want kids and you definitely don't, for instance), it's probably worth it to go out again even if you feel a bit "meh" after the first outing. At best, you'll find that you two are more compatible than you realized, at worst, you'll get more experience practicing mindfulness and interpersonal skills while dating. Do remember to communicate with your date when you know you aren't interested, so you don't inadvertently string them along or send them mixed signals.

Do you often continue feeling ambivalent several weeks into dating? This might indicate a pattern of perfectionism or avoidant attachment. If you find yourself analyzing every detail about the person and looking for reasons to end things in order to avoid some future incompatibility, practice mindfulness skills to come back to the reality as it is now. Return to Katz's questions about your mate: do you have fun with them, can you be yourself, are you attracted to them, do they make an effort to communicate and spend time with you, are your values and goals aligned? There will always be some amount of risk in any relationship, and every potential partner will have quirks or flaws we need to learn to live with and adapt to.

Dating apps make it seem like there are endless options. For some, that means it is hard to decide to commit to the great option in front of them, for fear that there may be someone better. From afar, someone else may look appealing, up close, as Dr. Stan Tatkin says, everyone is high maintenance.[31] If indecision is distressing and checking the facts does not quell the angst, do some self-soothing or get out emotional energy through intense activity. If the thoughts are overwhelming, try to distract by focusing your mind on a new mental challenge. Give your brain something else to problem solve besides your love life. Our minds can help us be discerning and make safe and healthy choices, but when we get into obsession and rumination for fear of making the wrong choice, our suffering is now not due to the relationship, but our fixation on it and desire to avoid pain.

Overanalyzing can be a form of hypervigilance, where the brain is scanning for threats and wants to feel safe. Practice *Loving-kindness* towards the parts that want to know you will be safe. Remember the resources that will help you cope with and overcome challenges when they come.

Pain and discomfort are a part of life and relationships. We must accept some risk and uncertainty in the future. So, try to trust what is truly good now, and allow life to unfold. *Radically accept* that we cannot know the future and cannot always prevent emotional pain.

Touch into *Wise Mind* to confirm you are on a path that feels right for you now and turn the volume down on emotion mind's fear-based attempts to predict the future.

**We've been seeing each other for ___ amount of time but I don't know if we're exclusive.**

If you and your date have been spending time together and increasing emotional or physical intimacy, it is reasonable and appropriate to ask about exclusivity. Asking for clarity about the status of your relationship or wanting to know how someone feels about you should not threaten the connection you have. If asking causes someone to label you as "needy," "clingy," or anything else negative, that is important information that lets you know this is someone who isn't comfortable having open and transparent discussions about your feelings, needs, and how the relationship experience is for you. A central part of intimacy is caring about each other's internal world—emotions, thoughts, desires, needs, dreams. Ask yourself if it works for you to have a partner who sees this as a big or unreasonable ask.

When someone likes you they will be excited to tell you or show you that, even if they aren't ready to be exclusive. If they aren't ready, *you get to decide* what you want and what you are comfortable with or willing to put up with.

Here's how you might use the *Interpersonal Effectiveness* skill of (O)DEAR MAN for this topic:

- Opener: (not technically a part of the skill, but a softer start up) Hey! I am glad we could catch up. It's really great to see you. I've been wanting to touch base with you about a few things.
- Describe the facts of the situation: We've been spending a lot of time together over the past several weeks. I know a few weeks ago we were both still on the apps and meeting with other people.
- Express your thoughts or feelings about it: I've really enjoyed getting to know you and feel we have a great connection and a lot of shared goals. I don't want to see anyone else at this point.
- Ask or Assert: I am curious where you're at with things now? Are you still dating other people?
- Reinforce: If you aren't at the same place I am, that's okay, but I would like to know if we both can see this being exclusive in the future.
- Mindfully express
- Appear confident
- Negotiate. For instance, if they need more time, give them a sense of your level of comfort with that: "Okay, I am happy to keep getting to know you for now. However, I don't feel comfortable getting more intimate than we have been while you still are seeing other people." Or "It seems like we are in really different places, and I think I need to step away from our connection for now, since I am wanting a monogamous long-term relationship, and it sounds like you aren't comfortable being exclusive any time soon."

**Follow? Friend? Like, share, retweet?**

If you're thinking about connecting with a romantic interest you've recently met on social media, first pause, and check in with *Wise Mind*.

While people have different levels of comfort around this, there are plenty of good reasons to not add Facebook/Insta/Twitter or your other online profiles into the mix until a connection is more established. At some point it makes sense to connect across these social accounts but consider whether you want someone you barely know to access a lot of info about you so quickly.

For some of us, our social media has been documenting our personal history, past relationships, or our private emotions that we share with our online friends. It is reasonable to hold off from inviting someone to delve into that within a few weeks of knowing you. Personally, I enjoy learning about someone else the old-fashioned way—through conversation and quality time spent together. Letting things unfold organically as you exchange stories and share your histories puts all the social media stuff in a more holistic context and helps to pace intimacy appropriately.

Also think about how you might handle this online connection if things don't pan out in a few dates. It can be tricky to navigate whether to block/mute/unfriend, and the longer you wait to see what the status of your connection will be, the less frequently this scenario will come up.

**Pacing sex while dating—do we do it or do we wait?**

There is no set timeline to determine when sexual intimacy will be right for you and your partner. Sex can mean any kind of physical touch or activity that involves sexual pleasure, and it will be up to you and your partner to have open and honest conversations about readiness, kinks and curiosities, and safer sex. It's not uncommon that the more emotional intimacy there is, the more ease and comfort there is in showing up vulnerably and proactively voicing desires, which can lead to greater enjoyment for all involved.

One aspect to be mindful of is whether sexual intimacy will intensify your attachment and whether that will match where you and your date are emotionally and intellectually. Of course, for some, sex is what helps build the emotional closeness, and may help bring that sense of ease in showing up for all the other stuff. Do what's right for you and your boo. If you two haven't discussed expectations around sex beforehand, there can be unintentional hurt feelings in the aftermath. For some, sex is a milestone of deepening the relationship, and with that, they want more contact or emotional closeness afterwards. For others, sex is another way of connecting but does not signal any shift in the dynamic. Discuss what sex means to each of you and share what expectations go along with increased physical intimacy. If you don't feel ready to have a conversation about sex, that might be a good cue to wait until you do to be intimate.

Above all, check in to see if sexual intimacy is being propelled by *Wise Mind* or emotion mind. If there is any pressure, feeling like you "should" be ready or fear that delaying intimacy will mean losing the relationship, that is emotion mind. Likewise, if there is any shame response to feeling ready and desiring consensual sex, thoughts of I "should" wait based on perceived outside judgment, that is also emotion mind. Only you can know what is best for your emotional and physical health.

What does Wise Mind say about what sexual intimacy means to you?

______________________________________________

______________________________________________

______________________________________________

What is your readiness for sexual intimacy? How do you know when you are ready?

______________________________________________

______________________________________________

______________________________________________

Nervous about broaching sex? Try to bring it up in a light-hearted way while feeling relaxed and flirtatious with your date. Texting about the topic can also be a comfortable way to open the discussion. Many people put some of this info right in their online profile—identifying themselves as queer, kinky, ace, etc, which can be a used as a jumping off point for conversation.

If the topic can be addressed in a way that feels organic and casual, rather than an out of the blue interrogation, it will put both of you at ease. You can use DEAR MAN if that's helpful, but it's also okay to treat sexual preferences as you would any other –we ask people about their favorite foods and music, it's totally healthy to expect that people also have and want to share their favorite sexual activities and fantasies. Of course, we want to gauge whether it's appropriate to go there based on the degree of openness and vulnerability we've been building with someone. It could be asking, "What do you enjoy in the bedroom?" or "Do you have a favorite sex toy?" or "Is sex an important part of a relationship for you?"

Exploring sexual compatibility is as valid as making sure our emotional and communication styles are compatible, and the conversation can create trust to make physical intimacy more comfortable and satisfying. Try to be non-judgmental and validating since people can feel vulnerable sharing some of their sexual desires. I think Dan Savage's GGG policy is a great guide for healthy and affirming sexual connection. In his words: "Think good in bed, giving based on a partner's sexual interests, and game for anything — within reason."[32]

For some situations, *DEAR MAN* might feel like a helpful way to prepare your words.

**D**escribe the facts, **E**xpress how you're feeling, **A**ssert/ask for what you need from them, **R**einforce if it feels appropriate. Be **M**indful, **A**ct Confident even if you're nervous, and **N**egotiate your differing preferences and needs. Some examples: "Things have been heating up between us and I am really attracted to you. I did want to check in about our STI status before things get too steamy. I got tested last month and everything was negative, but I have had HPV in the past. I can answer any questions you have about that. Have you gotten tested recently?" While reinforcing isn't necessary at this stage, it could be added to encourage someone, as in, "I'm excited to rip your clothes off once you get your results" or "once you pick up those condoms we can really get things going." Another example: "Now that we've been dating for a few weeks, I wanted to let you know I do need to take things slowly. I feel nervous talking about it, but because I have had some bad experiences in the past, I need time to build trust before taking things to the next level sexually. I hope you can understand and be patient as I get more comfortable. I am really into you and just need some time." How someone responds to your sexual needs and interests, and how willing they are to have mature and open conversation will indicate their capacity develop a fulfilling physical relationship.

**She's/He's/They're great, but I'm still super anxious!**

If someone you're dating is consistently communicating and actively showing interest and you are still feeling anxious, it could be that a stress response gets activated when you start to have feelings for someone due to a past insecure relational experience. Do what you can to be dialectical: accept that you feel this way, give yourself compassion while also working to change or at least not act on this feeling.

*STOP skill*—this skill reminds us to:

- Stop, before acting on any emotions.
- Take a step back, take a few slow deep belly breaths, making the exhale longer than the inhale.
- Observe your emotions, sensations, and thoughts mindfully and notice what is happening around you. Very likely, you are safe, and nothing is urgent even if the feeling in your body is making you feel that way.
- Proceed mindfully. This may mean practicing some other skills like distract or self-soothe to cope and find calm until you know what action to take in your dating life.

*TIPP skills*

Sometimes when we are super anxious or on the verge of panic, it can feel impossible to mentally shift. When our body is flooded with intense distress, we can make changes to our biology to help manage anxiety's physiological effects. If you need a major reset, try one of the TIPP skills. They can be fast and effective ways to reduce emotional intensity.

- Temperature—extreme cold can bring down heart rate and blood pressure quickly, which will bring relief from a heightened emotional state. Some options: hold your breath and dip your face in ice-cold water for 30 seconds. Or tilt your head down slightly while holding an ice pack on your eyes and cheeks for 30 seconds.. If you have any cardiac concerns, consult with a doctor first to make sure this is a safe option for you.
- Intense exercise—expel emotions, tire yourself out, and reset your nervous system with 20 minutes of aerobic activity. Oxygen flow will help anxiety go, and the neuromodulators that are released during and after this kind of physical activity often bring feelings of peace and contentment.
- Paced Breathing—pace your breathing by intentionally slowing it down, be mindful and count 4-5 seconds as you inhale, then count as you exhale for 6-7 seconds. Find the combination that works for you. Heart rate drops as we breathe out, so make that exhale a couple seconds longer than the in-breath.
- Progressive Muscle Relaxation—this exercise is based on a simple principle of tensing and tightening muscle groups one at a time and then releasing them and has been found to reduce anxiety and stress. Here's how you do it:

    1. Breathe in while you tighten and contract one muscle group (start with the feet and ankles) for 5-10 seconds, then suddenly release and exhale.
    2. Relax for moment and repeat this first step, moving onto the calves, upper legs and thighs, glutes, stomach, back, chest, lower and upper arms, hands and wrists, shoulders, neck, jaw and lips, eyes and cheeks, forehead.
    3. Tighten, hold for 5-10 seconds, then release and shake loose between each group.
    4. As you gradually work your way through tensing then relaxing your body, notice the small changes.

*PLEASE CAN skills*—Speaking of biology, our mental health can be negatively impacted by lack of sleep or skipping nutritious meals. Return to the basics of self-care and the daily routines that help you feel your best. A reminder that my version of the PLEASE skills are:

- Physical health—take medications as prescribed, treat illness, be proactive about going to medical appointments and checkups, do what you need to feel healthy.
- Light in the morning—get natural light every morning by going outside for 10-20 minutes.
- Eat nutritious and delicious foods that make you feel good.
- Avoid substances that disrupt sleep or alter your mood or increase anxiety
- Sleep 8 hours and establish a nightly routine to wind down, avoid all light from 10pm-4am.
- Exert yourself or move for fun each day.

Is there anything you can do to improve your PLEASE skills?

___

___

*CAN skill*—I'm throwing in another acronym that I made up because I CAN. :-) The CAN skill means that you focus on being around people and doing activities that are Centering, Affirming, and Nurturing. Take a moment to write out who those people and what those activities are for you?

___

---

---

**She's/He's/They're great but I still feel the urge to leave sometimes!**

When we recognize that running or retreating from intimacy is part of our pattern, we can make the choice to cope with urges without acting upon them, to start to disrupt and transform our habits that undermine the goal of having a long-term relationship.

In DBT, the Distress Tolerance module includes strategies to survive a difficult emotional state. We might not necessarily feel better while practicing these skills. The goal is not to improve our mood, although it's nice if that happens. The main priority is to stop ourselves from acting on impulse or do anything that we might regret or that would make things worse.

Distress Tolerance skills like *ACCEPTS* can include activities that get your mind off stressful thoughts, or sensory experiences that are soothing—or jolting—and bring your nervous system down a couple notches from fight or flight.

The *TIPP* skills, like cold temperature, through an ice-cold shower or an ice pack on the cheeks and eyes can be a fast way to reduce the heart rate and help us feel calmer. Intense exercise can help us expend agitated energy and offer a healthy outlet for strong emotions.

What are some other ways you can tolerate the discomfort of being vulnerable around someone and beginning to trust and rely on someone, if that is generally a scary place for you? Can you think of some effective tools to survive an unpleasant feeling without acting on the impulse to do something drastic to get rid of it? This could include breathing techniques, movement or mindfulness practices, mantras, exercise, or other engaging and distracting activities.

______________________________________________

______________________________________________

It might also be helpful to practice the Pros and Cons skill from the Distress Tolerance module. Here we consider the advantages and disadvantages of using our skills, as well as the advantages and disadvantages or not using our skills. Notice how I have filled out the Pros and Cons chart and see if you can come up with the pros and cons for your situation.

| | *Using Distress Tolerance skills* | *Not using Distress Tolerance skills* |
|---|---|---|
| PROS | I am less likely to make a rash decision about my relationship. I can be sure to use Wise Mind rather than emotion mind to deal with relationship issues. | It seems like leaving the relationship would be easier and might bring relief quickly. |
| | *Using Distress Tolerance skills* | *Not using Distress Tolerance skills* |
| CONS | It is really hard work to use my skills and takes a lot of mindfulness and can feel really tiring | This experience will probably come up in any relationship, so if I leave I will face this again in the future.<br>There are a lot of positives about this relationship I would be sad to lose if I act on my urges. |

Your turn:

| | *Using Distress Tolerance skills* | *Not using Distress Tolerance skills* |
|---|---|---|
| PROS | | |
| | *Using Distress Tolerance skills* | *Not using Distress Tolerance skills* |
| CONS | | |

When we identify the pros of acting on urges, we can brainstorm other strategies that can offer similar benefits. Are the pros of acting on our urges short or long-term? Are the pros of using skills more consistent with our values? Are the cons of not using skills more detrimental to us?

*Interpersonal Effectiveness*—Navigating our needs around attachment will not only mean we have to use Distress Tolerance skills, but we may also have to communicate those needs or request some understanding, patience, or space if we need to step back to do our internal work.

Interpersonal Effectiveness skills first ask us to define our priorities. Identify your goals: to get what you want, to preserve your relationship, to stand up for your needs. Many times, it will be a combination of all three. If you want to maintain the relationship, but also want your needs to be heard and respected, balance a soft and validating tone towards your mate, with a steady resolve to commit to your needs.

The basic template for asking for something we need still works here:

- **D**escribe the facts of the situation
- **E**xpress your thoughts or feelings about it
- **A**sk or Assert
- **R**einforce what's in it for them
- **M**indfully express
- **A**ppear confident
- **N**egotiate

To amp up the assertiveness, add the *FAST* skills: Be **F**air to yourself and the other person, Don't **A**pologize for having needs, **S**tick to your values, be **T**ruthful. To make sure the other person feels good about the interaction, use the *GIVE* skills: approach in a **G**entle manner, act **I**nterested in their perspective, **V**alidate what they are feeling, and keep an **E**asy manner.

This might sound like: "We've been spending a lot of time together and I really care about you. I am realizing, though, that I need a little time to work through some old stuff that is coming up for me, so I am going to take the next week to myself. I know it's probably hard hearing this, and it's not personal. In any relationship I need to make sure I am getting enough space. I want our relationship to last and that means we'll need to figure out a schedule that works for us both."

Do your best to communicate from a place of integrity, in accordance with your own values, being fair, kind, and clear. If a partner responds in a way that feels unsupportive, is focused on their fears of rejection or abandonment, you can try to validate their emotions while repeating your need and reminding them of what is in it for them. However, you cannot both people-please and set boundaries at the same time. You don't have to fix anyone's feelings, and there is no way to ensure that someone won't be hurt. If someone continues to react negatively to such a request, all you can do is practice tolerating the discomfort of seeing someone else having emotions, continue to express understanding of how they feel, while still advocating for what you need. This skill is called *Broken Record*, where we calmly re-state our position.

A relationship has to work for both parties involved. Ask yourself how much you are willing to negotiate and set boundaries. Consider couples counseling if there is a push-pull dynamic of a pursuing partner and a distancing partner that is causing frequent tension and conflict. If someone expresses disappointment but still shows understanding, do your best to show empathy for the hurt without changing or apologizing for your needs.

If you are the one receiving a request for space, work to connect to the needs of the person you care about and offer support while coming back with your own request—this could be wanting a call or check in during their time alone, or a negotiated schedule with some guaranteed days together and other days where you can be apart. You can decide if this works for you. If it doesn't work, communicate that clearly and calmly without interpreting their need for space as an attack. This could simply be: "In a relationship I really need consistent communication at least every couple of days." Do notice if fears of rejection or a story about this being abandonment are activated by past situations rather than the current dynamics.

**It is okay to have needs! Resisting the urge to appease or avoid conflict.**

Continuously appeasing someone to avoid a conflict or disappointing them is a recipe for disaster. Swallowing and shutting down your own emotions and needs will likely lead to resentment and will also mislead your partner to believe everything is fine when it is not.

If the avoidance of asking for what you need is rooted in fear of losing the relationship, work to radically accept that you could survive a loss of a connection if it meant being authentic and standing up for yourself. If you are trying to avoid feeling shame when a partner expresses hurt feelings or disappointment when you express a need that conflicts with their wishes, build tolerance to hold space for someone's pain without needing to fix or rescue them from it, and without taking on their feelings on as your responsibility. Sometimes the best way of showing up is to witness the pain, validate it, while also standing your ground. Both things can be done.

*Observe* the emotions you are feeling and any urges to fix or rescue. Practice noticing how the other person is responding, how you are feeling, without judging or reacting.

The *STOP skill* might come in handy if your fear conflict and tend to feel overwhelmed when someone else responds with sadness or anger to a boundary or need you communicate.

- Stop
- Take a few breaths/Take a step back
- Observe your thoughts, feelings, the situation non-judgmentally
- Proceed Mindfully.

Sometimes that mindful step we can take is just to have a time out from a tense conversation and to come back to it later. Don't keep putting off or delaying your needs. Practice stating what you need clearly, kindly, and calmly, and accepting if someone doesn't like the situation. It's up to them to set their own boundaries about what they need in response, and up to you to decide whether the relationship is right for you if they are not appropriate, make threats to end things, or show contempt.

Interpersonal Effectiveness can provide a guide to get through the tension of conflicting needs. The *GIVE* skill asks us to be **G**entle, act **I**nterested in the other person's experience and perspective, **V**alidate their feelings, and have an **E**asy manner. The *FAST* skill reminds us to be **F**air to ourselves and the other person, to not **A**pologize for having reasonable needs, to **S**tick to our values, and be **T**ruthful.

Remember that you have the right to express your emotions and needs, to ask for help or support, to have your own feelings, opinions, and beliefs even if others do not understand them, to say "no," to put yourself first sometimes, to advocate for yourself, and to set boundaries even if that is hard for someone to accept.

**Uh-oh! We had our first fight.**

Don't let the fact that you and your new sweetie had an argument discourage you too much. Conflict that is approached in a healthy and constructive way is a normal part of any intimate relationship. It isn't whether you fight but how you fight that matters.

Focus on bringing a team mindset to issues that come up—meaning, find a way to side with your partner so that you work together to solve a problem. Assume the best about each other's intentions. State your complaints about specific behaviors rather than criticize your partner or make judgments about their character traits. For instance, "You've been 20 minutes late the last 3 times we were scheduled to meet. I feel frustrated and want to figure out how we can get on the same page about schedules."

This has a much gentler, kinder, and more collaborative approach in contrast to: "You never show up on time and it's selfish of you to not consider my needs. I wish you would stop being so irresponsible." If things get heightened and voices raised it will be crucial to offer what the Gottmans call "repair attempts," that demonstrate your care for your significant other.[33] This can be a gesture or statement that softens the interaction and re-connects you to each other, and it can be helpful to check in before a fight to see what kinds of things each of you might receive well—for some a joke will lighten the mood, and for others it will come off as minimizing the situation.

Some individuals experience physiological flooding during disagreements. People with a trauma history can be more prone to hypervigilance in detecting threat and then misperceive cues during a tense moment with a partner. This can activate the sympathetic nervous system's fight, flight, or freeze response, while simultaneously slowing down functioning of the pre-frontal cortex. Take a time-out if either of you are overwhelmed and moving into shut down or activation. Try some *self-soothe* strategies that use the senses to unwind or the *TIPP skills* to downshift the nervous system.

DEAR MAN can help guide difficult conversations so that you both are able to hear and respect what the other is feeling and needing.

CHAPTER FOUR

# *Final Thoughts*

## In a Relationship?

If a few dates led to a few more, and the weeks turned into months with a special someone, good for you! I hope you feel proud of yourself for communicating your needs and building a positive mutual connection grounded in your Wise Mind.

Continue tuning in with your *Wise Mind* as you reach milestones and progress in the relationship. Periodically review the emotions you identified as essential to a healthy relationship and see how aligned this connection is to those feelings.

*Healthy Relationship Emotions*

Alive—you feel vibrant and open to life and new experiences in your relationship

Calm—there is a quality of feeling at peace and soothed in your relationship

Comfortable—you can be yourself with your partner and feel at ease

Confident—you feel sure of yourself and know that you matter and have a lot to offer

Centered—you are grounded and trust yourself to make good decisions

Excited—you look forward to spending time with your partner and achieving dreams together

Expansive—you have a sense of relaxation and trust in life and the future about your relationship

Free—you feel able to explore and grow as an individual even while in partnership

Grateful—you feel fulfilled and appreciative that this person is in your life

Grounded—you feel mindful and are secure in the connection to yourself and partner

Inspired—you feel connected to your creativity and moved to self-expression

Joyful—you experience laughter, delight, and openness together

Loved/Loving—you feel warmth and affection towards your partner and experience those in return

Motivated—the relationship encourages you to move towards your goals and you feel energized

Passionate—your relationship allows you to express desires and experience sensual excitement

Proud—you feel a sense of achievement and contentment in who you are and the life you've led

Safe—you feel secure and able to show up vulnerably in your relationship

Stimulated—you feel intellectually challenged and engaged

Strong—you feel capable, determined, and empowered in your body

Turned on—you are attracted to your partner and enjoy exploring and expressing your sexuality with them

*Troubled Relationship Emotions*

Addicted—you feel a sense of urgency and craving for contact when apart from your partner

Afraid—you feel on edge and worry about angering your partner

Anger—you experience intense feelings when things don't go your way or as you hoped they would

Annoyed—you feel impatient and upset around your partner or when thinking about them

Anxious—you worry about losing the relationship if you don't say or do the "right" thing or worry about losing yourself by getting too close to your partner

Appalled—you feel shocked at their behaviors towards you or others

Bored—you feel uninspired and disconnected with your partner

Confused—you feel ambivalence towards your partner or don't know the status of your relationship and wonder how your partner truly feels about you

Contempt—you are feeling resentful or starting to think negatively about who your partner is as a person

Disappointment—you feel hurt or letdown by your partner's actions or inaction

Disconcerted—you have concerns about your relationship and feel unsettled

Disoriented—sometimes you don't know what is real or not, you feel like you can't always trust your own version of events and feel lost during conversations or conflict with your partner

Dread—you feel apprehensive and experience negative anticipation before conversations or interactions with your partner

Guilt—you feel a sense of responsibility for your partner's well-being and worry you aren't doing enough for them

Exhausted—you feel tired from emotional ups and downs or from not taking proper care of your basic needs

Flooded—you feel overwhelmed with intense sensation or emotion

Inadequate—you worry that you are not "good enough" for your partner and feel less than

Insecure—you don't trust the relationship can endure conflict or worry that your partner may leave at any time

Isolated—you find yourself feeling alone and reluctant or unable to reach other to others outside your relationship

Jealous—you feel suspicious of your partner's other relationship or insecure about their past relationships

Lonely—you don't feel known or seen in your relationship and long for more intimacy

Sad—you experience hurt from not having needs met

Shame—you feel like there is something wrong with you that is causing the issues in your relationship, or believe that if you left there would be no one else to love you

Stressed—you find you are in *fight, flight, or freeze* a lot in your relationship

Ask yourself whether the feelings that are present are due to actual behaviors and experiences with your mate. In the past, I had romantic feelings for a partner and clung onto the idea that we were meant to be together, even as he grew increasingly physically and emotionally distant and was chronically focused on himself. Even though I felt "in love," if I had taken stock, I would have noticed that underneath that, I felt lonely, confused, inadequate, and exhausted much of the time.

*How can you protect yourself from an unhealthy relationship masked by the rush of romantic feelings?*

1. Identify your emotions. Compare the reality of your relationship with what you had hoped for. There doesn't need to be an exact match but having most of the words from the healthy emotion list and few to none from the troubled relationship list is what to look for.

2. Have a few trusted friends who will give you honest feedback. It may take some outside input to help wake you up to what is happening in your relationship and to what emotions you are regularly experiencing. Be willing to take in perspectives on how your relationship is impacting you, especially if multiple people you trust are expressing similar worries. Notice if you tend to make excuses or defend your connection as "special" or "magical."

3. Check the facts.

What are the *specific* actions and behaviors that you and your partner do in your relationship that contribute to positive emotions? What are the *specific* ways that your partner and your relationship meet your needs?

______________________________________________

______________________________________________

______________________________________________

______________________________________________

When you partner has done something hurtful, did they take responsibility and express empathy for how it impacted you? Did they apologize and change their behavior?

______________________________________________

______________________________________________

______________________________________________

Do you both openly share your emotions with each other, and do you both feel comfortable expressing your needs?

______________________________________________

4. Review what needs are being met in your relationship. If there are other important needs of yours that are not being met in your primary partnership, but are fulfilled by other aspects of life, note that. Look for needs that are a priority for a romantic relationship that feel neglected and see if you need to address this with your partner or shift something about your own behavior to make this happen.

ACCEPTANCE, AFFECTION, APPRECIATION, BELONGING, COOPERATION, COMMUNICATION, CLOSENESS, COMMUNITY, COMPANIONSHIP, COMPASSION, CONNECTION, CONSIDERATION, CONSISTENCY, EMPATHY, INCLUSION, INTIMACY, LOVE, NURTURING, RESPECT, SAFETY, SECURITY, SEXUAL INTIMACY, STABILITY, SUPPORT, TO KNOW AND BE KNOWN, TO SEE AND BE SEEN, TO UNDERSTAND AND BE UNDERSTOOD, TRUST, WARMTH, HONESTY, AUTHENTICITY, INTEGRITY, PRESENCE, PLAY, JOY, HUMOR, EQUALITY, FAIRNESS, MUTUALITY, HARMONY, INSPIRATION, ORDER, CHOICE, FREEDOM, INDEPENDENCE, SPACE, SPONTANEITY, CHALLENGE, CLARITY, COMPETENCE, CONTRIBUTION, CREATIVITY, EFFICACY, GROWTH, HOPE, LEARNING, PARTICIPATION, PURPOSE, SELF-EXPRESSION, TO MATTER

5. Also check to make sure you and your partner are creating a life that is true to your values and priorities. Reflect again on what your values are and compare to the

values expressed by you and your partnership. If you see something concerning here, it is important to talk with your partner about it, using the ODEAR MAN skills, or if you want extra support, by meeting with a couples' therapist or counselor.

*Values and Priorities*

Connection—have close and satisfying friendships, feel a sense of belonging, give and receive affection and love, have and keep close friends, spend time with family members, have people with whom to do activities, show up as a present and engaged friend, partner, family member, etc., be receptive to feedback and work through challenges that arise in relationships, spend quality time with people I care about, end destructive relationships

Leadership— have authority over systems or an organization, manage and lead people, decide how resources are used, be respected by others, be seen as successful and obtain recognition, be competitive with others

Creativity—use the arts to express the inner self, learn, practice, and hone a creative talent, view the world through a lens of art and poetry, innovate and use the imagination, engage the senses

Goal-oriented— achieve significant goals, be involved in important projects, be productive, work hard, be ambitious, keep growing and improving in life

Pleasure— have an enjoyable time, seek fun activities and things that offer satisfaction, have ample free time, enjoy my work, relax and vacation

Adventure— try new and different things in life, be daring seek out exciting events relationships and things, enjoy high-sensation activities, travel and explore

Tradition— practice humility and modesty, follow traditions and customs, respect authority and follow rules, treat others well, follow through on responsibilities and obligations

Autonomy— follow my own path in life, be self-directed, make my own decisions and feel free, be independent, take care of myself and those I'm responsible for, have freedom of thought and action, act in terms of my own priorities

Spirituality— live life according to spiritual principles, practice a faith or religion, gain an understanding of myself and my life's spiritual purpose, understand and do the will of God or higher consciousness and find spiritual or divine meaning in life

Stability— live in secure and safe environment, basically healthy and fit, prioritize mental health and wellness, have a steady income that meets my own and my family's needs

Compassion— be fair, treat people equally and provide equal opportunities, understand different people, be open minded, care for nature and the environment, be a steward of the land, consider others

Service— help people or animals in need, care for others' well-being and improve society, be committed to a cause or to a group that has a larger purpose beyond my own, donate time or money or effort, be committed to a group that shares my beliefs and values, find a calling that is in service to a higher good or well-being of a community

Personal growth— self-development, adhere to a personal philosophy of life, learn and do challenging things that help me grow and mature as a human, get out of my comfort zone, and test limits, exercise a growth mindset and be willing to struggle to learn new things

Integrity—acknowledge and stand up for my personal beliefs, be an honest and responsible person and keep my word to others, be courageous in facing and living life, be a person who pays debts to others and repairs damage I've caused, be accepting of myself, others, and life as it is, live without resentment, be willing to do the right thing even when it is hard

**Still single?**

For as long as you are single, or if you find yourself there unexpectedly again, remember that being unpartnered is a valid and whole human experience.

It is reasonable to long for someone with whom to share your life, and to wish to experience intimacy and delight in a loving relationship. Still, anchor yourself in all the ways you are wonderfully you as a friend, family member, pet parent, enthusiast of your interests and achiever of your unique dreams.

If you need a boost, complete a free survey at https://www.viacharacter.org/ and learn more about what your strengths are.

Practice *loving-kindness* towards yourself and others.

Reflect on how you can help other people who are alone feel less lonely, and I bet they will return that energy. Show up as a loving and caring friend, and those friendships will provide support and fulfillment. Contribute to a cause that you believe in and find yourself an important part of a web of people and beings, adding goodness into the world and reaping the rewards of community involvement.

Continue to participate fully in your life and meet others doing the same. I truly believe that when we pursue our authentic path, we meet the people we need and who can help us grow and experience joy, whether that's in a romantic relationship, or platonic.

# DBT FOR DATING PLAYLIST

*I Need Somebody to Love Tonight* –Sylvester
*I Wanna Be Down* –Brandy
*The Sexy Getting Ready Song* –Rachel Bloom
*Phone Down* –Erykah Badu
*Could We* –Cat Power
*Shut Up Kiss Me* –Angel Olsen
*Latch* –Disclosure featuring Sam Smith
*Kissability* –Sonic Youth
*Wrecking Ball* –Miley Cyrus
*Loud Places* –Jamie xx, Romy
*No Romance* –Tirzah
*Call Me Maybe* –Carly Rae Jepsen
*A Long Walk* –Jill Scott
*When I Think of You* –Janet Jackson
*Oh, To Be in Love* –Kate Bush
*Nite and Day* –Meshell Ndegeocello
*All the Way Down* –Kelela
*Die Hard* –Kendrick Lamar
*Ex-Factor* –Lauryn Hill
*Since I Left You* –The Avalanches
*Needed Me*—Rihanna
*Fire* -Waxahatchee
*Dream* –Madison McFerrin featuring Photay

## ACKNOWLEDGEMENTS

So many made this workbook possible!

First and foremost, thank you to Dr. Marsha Linehan for developing Dialectical Behavior Therapy.

Dr. Jeanette Sarbo and Dr. Kristi Webb, your DBT groups improved my quality of life exponentially and made me fall in love with the skills.

Tremendous thanks to Alex and Lindsey and the entire Tiny Book Course team for guidance, encouragement, and to Tracie, for your incredibly helpful edits, advice, and feedback. You 100% helped me "get it done!" My fellow TBC authors, our co-working sessions kept me focused and accountable. You rock!

Dr. Nicole Childs and Kit Nowell, LMFT, thank you for reading drafts and for your invaluable suggestions—I so appreciate your wisdom and expertise, as well as your wonderful friendship.

To mom, for catching those superfluous commas and run-on sentences.

To Dr. Marc Grimmett, thank you for being a genuine, compassionate, bold soul, and for supporting my dreams.

To my past partners, our experiences, good and bad, helped inform the content here.

I am grateful for the circumstances that motivated me to write this workbook. I am thankful I was able to turn anguish into action, and to find freedom and relief on the other side. May others learn what love is—and isn't—in less painful ways.

Marja and dad, thank you for a soft place to land and for forest walks, pulla at Café Zoceria, and a sauna/cold plunge experience of a lifetime.

Marie, Sophie, Mathilde, and Alta: our hikes through alpine meadows, dips in glacial lakes, chats and laughs among moose and mountain goats brought me back to life. I am so grateful we shared the Glacier experience together. What joy—it boosted and energized me to get to the finish line.

My friendships are where I've felt the most enduring and consistent love. Beautiful Alexandra, thank you for being on the DBT journey with me, for your vulnerability, kindness, and care, and for riffing title ideas with me. Courtney, I appreciate your sass, strength, steady support, and virtual companionship. Amy, thanks for inspiration and modeling integrity, curiosity, and whole-hearted living. Huge thanks also to Sonoe, Tzu Chen, Shila, Tina Joy, Sarah, Rachelle, Marlon, Julie F., Julie H., Ellen, Jackie, and so many more...you all have cheered me on through life and during this project. Your faith in me helped me keep at it, more than you know.

Gratitude to my clients. You've shown up with courage, adaptability, and openness that makes our work together inspiring and instructive in my own life.

I've gotta shout out my dogs, Yoko and Rosie, as well, for staying by my side during long stretches at my laptop, getting me out for frequent walk breaks, and being so darn cute.

APPENDIX

# *DBT SKILLS*

From or adapted from Marsha Linehan's *DBT Skills Training Handouts and Worksheets.*[34]

**Skills to use when emotions are intense or super uncomfy—use these in order to not make things worse!**

*STOP skill*

Stop, before acting on any emotions.
Take a few slow deep belly breaths, making the exhale longer than the inhale.
Observe your emotions, sensations, and thoughts mindfully and notice what is happening around you. Very likely, you are safe, and nothing is urgent even if the feeling in your body is making you feel that way.
Proceed mindfully. This may mean practicing some other skills like distract or self-soothe to cope and find calm until you know what action to take in your dating life.

*TIPP skill*

Temperature—extreme cold (ice pack over eyes and cheeks, cold shower) can lower heart rate and reduce anxious feelings, extreme heat (sauna) has similar aftereffects as exercise, releasing endorphins, and preliminary studies link sauna use to a reduction in depressive symptoms[35]
Intense exercise—release endorphins and have a healthy outlet for strong emotions, regulate nervous system and heart rate through activity
Paced Breathing—lengthen and slow down the exhale to feel calmer, lengthen the inhale to feel more alert

Progressive Muscle Relaxation—tense up each muscle group, part by part, hold for several seconds then release

*Distract (ACCEPTS= Activities, Contribution, Compassion, Emotions, Push Away, Thoughts, Sensations) or Self-soothe*

Engage in fun, light, or engrossing activities that get your mind off the situation. Baking, roller skating, board games, crossword puzzles, knitting, dog walking, making art, putting a puzzle together, masturbating, dancing to your favorite songs, calling a friend, watching a movie, etc. You know best how you can distract yourself from negative self-talk or painful emotions. Self-soothing activities might be particularly helpful. Sipping hot cocoa, eating delish ice cream, taking a nap, taking a fragrant bath, or using aromatherapy, practicing visualization or guided meditation are just a few ideas to calm the nervous system.

*Radical Acceptance a process and practice of acknowledging* reality, no longer fighting what is. Some ways to practice:

- Notice that you are arguing with reality when you are in a story of "this shouldn't or can't be happening."
- Repeatedly say aloud or write down the difficult truth you are working to accept.
- Observe and allow the sensations and emotions that come up as you work towards acceptance.
- Imagine how would you act if you had accepted the reality and make choices and behave as if you already have accepted.
- Engage your body in the process: open your arms wide lift your chest up, tit your head to the sky and notice the sensation of surrendering to what is.
- Remind yourself that life can be meaningful and fulfilling even when we are experiencing rejection and hurt.

**Skills to use to have difficult conversations or to communicate your needs**

*DEAR MAN*

Opener
Describe the facts of the situation
Express your thoughts and feelings
Assert or Ask for what you want
Reinforce what's in it for them or what the consequence are
and do so Mindfully, Appear Confident, Negotiate
**GIVE**: If your main goal is preserving the relationship, be soft in your delivery and validate the other person's perspective.
**FAST**: If standing up for yourself is your main goal, be truthful, consistent with your values, and don't apologize for how you feel or what you need.

**Everyday maintenance and mindfulness skills—ongoing practice to build a meaningful life and to make wise decisions while dating**

*PLEASE CAN skills*

Physical health—take medications as prescribed, treat illness, be proactive about going to medical appointments and checkups, do what you need to feel healthy.

Light in the morning—get natural light every morning by going outside for at least 10 minutes.

Eat nutritious and delicious foods that make you feel good.

Avoid substances that disrupt sleep or alter your mood or increase anxiety

Sleep 8 hours and establish a nightly routine to wind down, avoid all light from 10pm-4am.

Exert yourself or move for fun each day.

And choose activities and to be around people that are:
Centering

Affirming
Nurturing
*VITALS—start something you are avoiding*

Validate
Imagine
Take the first small step
Applaud yourself
Lighten the load
Sweeten the deal

*Wise Mind*—the inner voice inside us all that knows what is best, the synthesis of reason and emotion

*What skills*—what we do when mindful: Observe, Describe, Participate
*How skills*—how we do the what skills: One-Mindfully, Non-Judgmentally, Effectively

*Observe*—witness and notice what you see, hear, taste, feel, etc. without labeling
*Describe*— put what you observe into non-judgmental words, state the facts
*Participate*—throw yourself fully into the moment, with alert, relaxed, and engaged attention

*One-Mindfully*— focus awareness on whatever you are doing in that moment, one thing at a time
*Non-judgmentally*— stop labeling experiences, ourselves, others, etc. as "good" or "bad" and instead note just the facts
*Effectively*— think about your goals and do what will work best to meet them and to let go of being "right"

*Mindfulness of Thoughts*—notice thoughts coming and going, without holding onto them, analyzing, or pushing away, allow them to pass, acknowledge without believing or reacting, be curious and hold thoughts loosely, try visualizing them as leaves floating down stream or clouds in the sky

*Mindfulness of Emotions*—notice emotions coming and going, as sensations or energy in the body, without holding onto them, judging, or pushing away, allow them to pass, acknowledge them without allowing them to control behaviors, be curious and hold space for emotions, imagine them as clouds passing in the sky, or as waves you are surfing

**Skills to regulate emotions**

*Check the facts*—distinguish between the facts of distressing events and your interpretations, record the who, what, where, what and remove any judgments, mind-reading, stories, and worst-case thinking
*Cope ahead*—even if the think you are imagining does happen, how would you cope? What are your inner and outer resources of support during a crisis? Imagine yourself coping successfully with various scenarios of situations going well or being challenging,
*Act as if*—embody the qualities you need to overcome a challenge, imagine you already knew you could overcome and act accordingly
*Opposite action of emotion urges*—if your emotions are based on interpretations rather than the facts of the situation, or if acting on your emotions won't be effective, identify the urges and act opposite of those urges

*Accumulating long-term positives*—remind yourself of your values, priorities, ethics, and act accordingly

*Loving-kindness*—a practice of directing compassion and warmth first to someone/animal easy to love, then directing this compassion to self, then others

*Walking the middle path, thinking dialectically*—avoid extremes and reconcile multiple truths that seem opposite—emotion and reason, acceptance, and change, allowing, respecting emotions, and not letting them control us, knowing this is hard and yet also that you are capable, closeness and autonomy, etc.

Space to write your thoughts and practice skills.

## *Recommended relationship, sex, & self-intimacy books*

Dodson, B. (1996). *Sex for one: The joy of self-loving.* Three Rivers Press.

Fern, J. (2022). *Polysecure: attachment, trauma and consensual non-monogamy.* Scribe Publications.

Fruzzetti, A. E. (2019). *The high-conflict couple: A dialectical behavior therapy guide to finding peace, intimacy & validation.* Echo Point Books & Media.

Gottman, J. M., & Silver, N. (2018). *The seven principles for making marriage work.* Cassell Illustrated.

Mariaskin, A. (2022). *Thriving in relationships when you have OCD: How to keep obsessions and compulsions from sabotaging love, friendship, and family connections.* New Harbinger Publications.

Moon, A. (2021). *Getting it: A guide to hot, healthy hookups and shame-free sex.* Ten Speed Press.

Nagoski, E. (2015). *Come as you are.* Simon & Schuster.

Perel, E. (2006). *Mating in captivity: Reconciling the erotic + the domestic.* HarperCollins.

Taitz, J. L. (2018). *How to be single and happy science-based strategies for keeping your sanity while looking for a mate.* A TarcherPerigee Book.

Tatkin, S. (2012). *Wired for Love how understanding your partner's brain can help you defuse conflicts and spark intimacy.* New Harbinger Publications.

Tawwab, N. G. (2021). *Set boundaries, find peace: A guide to reclaiming yourself.* A Tarcher Perigee book.

Ury, L. (2022). *How to not die alone: The surprising science that will help you find love.* Simon & Schuster Paperbacks.

## NOTES

[1] Linehan, M. M. (2008). Cognitive-behavioral treatment of borderline personality disorder. (pp. 126). TPB.

[2] Linehan, M. M. (2015). Rationale for Dialectical Behavior Therapy Skills Training. In DBT skills training manual. chapter, Guilford.

[3] Franzen, A. (2018, July 12). Go with you Hut [web log]. Retrieved September 11, 2022, from http://www.alexandrafranzen.com/2018/07/12/go-with-your-hut/.

[4] Linehan, M. (2015). DBT skills training handouts and worksheets. (pp. 51-52). The Guilford Press.

[5] Linehan, M. (2015). DBT skills training handouts and worksheets. (pp. 213). The Guilford Press.

[6] Lisitsa, E. (n.d.). The Four Horsemen: The Antidotes [web log]. Retrieved September 10, 2022, from https://www.gottman.com/blog/the-four-horsemen-the-antidotes/.

[7] The Center for Nonviolent Communication. Center for Nonviolent Communication. (2005). Retrieved September 10, 2022, from https://www.cnvc.org/

[8] Cadden, C., & Wiens, J. (2010). Welcome to ZENVC - ZENVC: The way with and without words. ZENVC. Retrieved September 10, 2022, from https://zenvc.org/

[9] Macias, A. (2014, May 28). 15 Pieces of Advice from Maya Angelou. Business Insider. Retrieved September 6, 2022, from

HTTPS://WWW.BUSINESSINSIDER.COM/MAYA-ANGELOU-QUOTES-2014-5.

[10] LINEHAN, M. (2015). DBT SKILLS TRAINING HANDOUTS AND WORKSHEETS. (PP. 253-255). THE GUILFORD PRESS.

[11] BROWN, B. (2017, DECEMBER 7). THE ONE PROBLEM WITH FEELING JOYFUL (AND HOW TO FIX IT). HUFFPOST. RETRIEVED OCTOBER 9, 2022, FROM HTTPS://WWW.HUFFPOST.COM/ENTRY/FINDING-HAPPINESS-BRENE-BROWN_N_4312653

[12] HUBERMAN, A. (2021, JANUARY). HUBERMAN LAB. MASTER YOUR SLEEP AND BE MORE ALERT WHEN AWAKE. PODCAST EPISODE.

[13] LINEHAN, M. (2015). DBT SKILLS TRAINING HANDOUTS AND WORKSHEETS. (PP. 344). THE GUILFORD PRESS.

[14] LINEHAN, M. (2015). DBT SKILLS TRAINING HANDOUTS AND WORKSHEETS. (PP. 253-255). THE GUILFORD PRESS.

[15] DE BOTTON, A. (2016, MAY 28). WHY YOU WILL MARRY THE WRONG PERSON. THE NEW YORK TIMES. RETRIEVED SEPTEMBER 10, 2022, FROM HTTPS://WWW.NYTIMES.COM/2016/05/29/OPINION/SUNDAY/WHY-YOU-WILL-MARRY-THE-WRONG-PERSON.HTML.

[16] BARTLETT, S., & HUSSEY, M. (2022, MAY 15). THE SECRET TO BUILDING A PERFECT RELATIONSHIP. THE DIARY OF A CEO. PODCAST EPISODE. RETRIEVED FROM HTTPS://PODCASTS.APPLE.COM/US/PODCAST/THE-DIARY-OF-A-CEO-WITH-STEVEN-BARTLETT/ID1291423644?I=1000560697259.

[17] URY, L. (2022). HOW TO NOT DIE ALONE: THE SURPRISING SCIENCE THAT WILL HELP YOU FIND LOVE. SIMON & SCHUSTER PAPERBACKS.

[18] MOORHEAD, M., SAFRANSKY, N., & WILKERSON, B. (1996). CHECK YOUR VITALS.

[19] SWOBODA, K. (N.D.). PRACTICING COURAGE [WEB LOG]. RETRIEVED SEPTEMBER 11, 2022, FROM HTTPS://WWW.YOURCOURAGEOUSLIFE.COM/BLOG/PRACTICING-COURAGE.

[20] Ury, L. (2022). How to not die alone: The surprising science that will help you find love. (pp. 171). Simon & Schuster Paperbacks.

[21] Ury, L. (2022). How to not die alone: The surprising science that will help you find love. (pp. 118-199). Simon & Schuster Paperbacks.

[22] Putnam, R. (2000). Bowling alone. Simon & Schuster.

[23] Jones, D. (2015, January 9). The 36 questions that lead to Love. The New York Times. Retrieved September 9, 2022, from https://www.nytimes.com/2015/01/09/style/no-37-big-wedding-or-small.html

[24] Bowen, L. (2020, September 18). The Diamond Dogs. Ted Lasso. episode, Apple TV+.

[25] Anderson, M., Vogels, E. A., & Turner, E. (2020, October 2). The virtues and downsides of online dating. Pew Research Center: Internet, Science & Tech. Retrieved October 6, 2022, from https://www.pewresearch.org/internet/2020/02/06/the-virtues-and-downsides-of-online-dating/

[26] Badu, E. (n.d.). Phone Down. On But you caint use my phone (mixtape). Motown (Capitol).

[27] Ury, L. (2022). How to not die alone: The surprising science that will help you find love. (pp. 171). Simon & Schuster Paperbacks.

[28] Franzen, A. (2018, July 12). Go with you Hut [web log]. Retrieved September 11, 2022, from http://www.alexandrafranzen.com/2018/07/12/go-with-your-hut/.

[29] Katz, E. M. (n.d.). Love U Podcast. episode. Retrieved 2014, from https://www.evanmarckatz.com/podcast. Permission for use granted by author in an email received September 8, 2022.

[30] Kabat-Zinn, J. (2014). In Wherever you go, there you are mindfulness meditation in everyday life (pp. 32). essay, Hachette Books.

[31] Tatkin, S. (2016) Wired for Dating. (pp. 89-90). New Harbinger.

[32] Dolan, E. W. (2015, April 16). Good, giving, and game: Research confirms that Dan Savage's sex advice works. PsyPost. Retrieved October 7, 2022, from https://www.psypost.org/2014/10/good-giving-game-research-confirms-dan-savages-sex-advice-works-28965

[33] Brittle, Z. (n.d.). R is for RepairZach. The Gottman Institute. Retrieved September 6, 2022, from https://www.gottman.com/blog/r-is-for-repair/

[34] Linehan, M. (2015). DBT skills training handouts and worksheets. The Guilford Press.

[35] Patrick, R. (2022, April 13). Sauna benefits deep dive and optimal use with Dr. Rhonda Patrick & medcram. FoundMyFitness. Retrieved September 9, 2022, from https://www.foundmyfitness.com/episodes/medcram-sauna

## ADDITIONAL REFERENCES


Karen, R. (1998). Becoming attached: First relationships and how they shape our capacity to Love. Oxford University Press.

Linehan, M. (2015). DBT skills training handouts and worksheets. The Guilford Press.

Linehan, M. M. (2015). DBT skills training manual. chapter, Guilford.

Tatkin, S. (2016) Wired for Dating. New Harbinger.

Printed in Great Britain
by Amazon